ENDOR᷈ ᷈᷈᷈ENTS

'Mark Stevens is no doubt a phenomenal minister of the Gospel. It's been my privilege and honour to know Mark for many, many years. He is an author, a psalmist, a musician, a singer, a pastor and a great expositor of the Word of God. Mark is one of those phenomenal last day singers with a true David's heart to minister through song in the anointing. His writing is insightful and deep, displaying kingdom truths that will penetrate the heart and cause change. His writing is accurate and will give you a sense of purpose and destiny as you read. Mark Stevens is a man who will continue to be mightily used by God around the nations and the world. I believe he has a Davidic last day worship calling to the body of Christ to call people into a place of knowing what it is to worship the Father in spirit and in truth. Those that know the Lord will worship him in spirit and in truth. So I can recommend this book as an incredible blessing to your life.'

Steve Maile
Oasis City Church, Watford

'Mark Stevens has been a blessing to the Body of Christ for more than twenty-five years. I have been aware of Mark's ministry over the years particularly in the area of praise and worship, where his songs and worship leading has had a wide impact on Christendom. Mark also communicates the Word of God with passion and effectiveness, rightly dividing the word of truth. Mark recently ministered at our church and we were very blessed; he has become a friend to me and I highly recommend this book and endorse his ministry.'

Bishop John Francis
Ruach City Church, London

'Mark Stevens' outstanding new book *This New Era* can be summed up in one line from a chapter late in the book: 'Birthing a New Era is not for the faint hearted!' Oh that is so true! I do believe we are standing at the turbulent threshold of a new era. Not only is Mark's writing packed with prophecy to inspire and direct, but the biblical grounding, storytelling and parables take the lessons we need to grasp to a whole new level. In any era-shift, you will face changing alignments, new methods, great conflict and much complexity, so whether you are a leader, influencer, a pastor or simply a quiet believer trying to understand how to bravely face the changing world around us, this is a must read!'

Jarrod Cooper
Revive Church, Hull

'The moment you open Mark's book *This New Era* you will find yourself entering the beautiful gate that will take you to a treasure chest: one that has all the prophetic revelations, wisdom and power keys to steer you through the uncertainties of the choppy waters so many are facing. Mark has packed into this brilliant book all the guidance and thrilling biblical illustrations you will ever need to flip any crisis into a game-changing eternal moment for you.

Jimi Dowds
Igniter of International Leaders, Dunfirmline

'In our post-pandemic world it's crucial that we apply the lessons we've learned and position ourselves and our churches for life in this new era. History is punctuated by striking events that shake and shift culture and values, and God invariably raises up visionary voices to lead a generation into its new season. Our world has undoubtedly changed, yet so many have returned to established patterns and habits in life and ministry. Mark's practical and prophetic appeal to locate ourselves in the flow of God's purposes for this new era is a timely reminder to allow God to punctuate his story through us.'

Mike McMahon
Urban Church, Warrington

'*This New Era* is not your average book on the shelf! This book is inspired and challenging, causing the reader to reach for more, to see beyond what you see now. The entire book is prophetic and and has clearly been birthed in Mark who has written a message that God has given him for every reader who picks this book up. *This New Era* has been beautifully and powerfully crafted and is the book you may not even know you need. It will change your future and generations to come. Well done on diligently serving God and ushering in this new era, Mark.'

Vicky Cross
Relentless Church, Warrington

'Mark Stevens has been a loyal and personal friend of mine for over fifteen years, We have journeyed through many seasons, learning God's ways, receiving revelation, gaining wisdom, insight and understanding regarding and interpreting the deep ways of God. I have watched, prayed and endeavoured to encourage Mark on his walk with the Lord and in paying a price for the call of God. The words of wisdom you will read in these pages carry not only information but an impartation of God's presence and a revelation of God's ways. Take this anointed sentence from this book for example. Within this sentence one senses a price paid, a revelation received, a word in season for 'Such a Time as This'. Here is the sentence: "I believe the call of the believer is to live with a sense of God-sight, to live with a sense of vision that supersedes, overwhelms, and overcomes its natural circumstances." *This New Era* is not for the faint hearted. This book is for the overcomers, the conquerors, it's for God's champions. Steve Jobs wrote these words: "The people who believe they can change the world are usually the ones that do." This book will fuel your vision to change your world and to change the world of others, it will give you 'God sight', it will speak to you prophetically and encourage your mind, soul and spirit to become one of God's champions in this next chapter on God's earth. Read this book prayerfully, for this is your time!'

John Edwards
Walking Free Ministries

•

'Spending time with Mark is a special experience. I've had the privilege of spending time with him on many occasions, both in intensity of church ministry and in the calm of simply hanging out. He is godly, insightful, fun, positive, courageous, wise, humble, purposeful, caring, genuine, and always, always, always looking forward. I've seen him move forward through the steps of change into new eras. I've seen him lead others forward through the steps of change into new eras. And he's walked with me as I have stepped forward through the steps of change into new eras. I have so many good things to say about this book. There is a ton of helpful material to draw from. And it's thoroughly rooted in the Bible. It's easy to endorse. But this book is not just about the words on the pages. It's the heartfelt call to "never stop looking forward to what God will do next" from a man who has lived and breathed the things he has written, and worked them out in the complexity of local church life. You are not simply buying a book, you are investing in the prophetic call from a genuine man of God who speaks from proven experience!'

Dave Akerman
LifeChurch, Warrington

'We haven't just entered a new season, but a whole new era. Everything has changed (or is changing) and the upheaval isn't anywhere near finished. *This New Era* is a book for such a time as this. My friend Mark Stevens has perceptively discerned the transitional juncture we are living in. He offers prophetic insights, biblical wisdom, and practical direction to help us navigate this uncharted territory. Through the exploration of characters such as David, Solomon, and Jacob, this book will equip you to flourish and advance in the midst of so much chaos and uncertainty. You will discover how to be positioned in the right place, with the right people, at the right time.'

Craig Cooney
Hope Church, Portadown, Co Armagh

'This book speaks with a prophetic voice announcing a new and glorious era for the church. It has been written with a deep biblical insight and real-world application. Mark Stevens communicates with a sense of urgency and those with a discerning heart need to pay careful attention to what the Spirit is saying to the present-day church. I am fully persuaded that reading this book will challenge, encourage, and transform your life.'

Dele Oderinde
The Kingdom Life Church, Preston

'Mark's book for me highlights the extent of his own relationship and growth in the Lord. God's Holy Spirit profoundly changed Mark's life some years ago and it is a true blessing to all who will read *This New Era* that since his first and deep experience with Jesus, Mark's overriding desire has been to share what the Lord has blessed him with. In this book he is strongly encouraging us all to seek a deeper relationship with God. The reader will discover many practical and realistic ways in which we can progress our own relationship with the God of creation that we serve, who loves us beyond measure. Dwelling on some of the relational and spiritual examples that Mark shares with us, I was led to consider the scripture that directs us to "seek and you will find". With the depth of experience that Mark shares with us in this book, he highlights the Lord's intention, that the more we seek the more we will find. Mark's experience with the Lord, reflected strongly in this book, is truly a work in rich spiritual progress that will benefit and encourage all who read it. As a born-again Christian of forty-four years I commend Mark's book to all that seek a closer relationship with our creator. If you know Jesus and seek to know Him more closely this is a book for you."

Errol Rendall
Rendall Ltd, Monaco

'*This New Era* is a timely encouragement that will resonate with individuals and churches who are grappling with transition and sense that it is far more than just a season change; they are stepping into a new era.'
Stephen Matthew
Church consultant, Building Church Academy

'I have known Mark for several years and have seen him actively engage in ministry. Every time I've met with him, I've come away with something powerfully prophetic and insightful in my life. *This New Era* is full of prophetic insights and I highly recommend it to you. You will come away with God's sight, not just eye-sight - something all of us need more of in our service for Christ and His body.'

Paul Hallam
Lighthouse Church, Salford and Manchester

THIS
NEW
ERA

THIS
NEW
ERA

A Collection of Prophetic Messages for the Church

Mark Stevens

Published in 2023 by Mark Stevens Music, Keighly, West Yorkshire, United Kingdom

The right of Mark Stevens to be identified as the author of this work has been asserted by her in accordance with the Copyright, Designs and Patents Act 1988. All rights reserved. No part of this publication may be reproduced or transmitted in any form or by any means, electronic or mechanical, including photocopy, recording or any information storage and retrieval system, without permission in writing from the publisher.

British Library Cataloguing in Publication Data. A catalogue record for this book is available from the British Library.

Design & Typesetting by Matt Lockwood, mattsstudio.co.uk

Unless otherwise stated, quotations from scripture are taken from the New King James Version®. Copyright © 1982 by Thomas Nelson. Used by permission. All rights reserved.

Scripture quotations marked KJV are from The Authorized (King James) Version: Rights in the Authorized Version in the United Kingdom are vested in the Crown. Reproduced by permission of the Crown's patentee, Cambridge University Press.

Scripture quotations marked TPT are from The Passion Translation®. Copyright © 2017, 2018, 2020 by Passion & Fire Ministries, Inc. Used by permission. All rights reserved. ThePassionTranslation.com.

ISBN-13: 978-1-3999-6158-5

CONTENTS

DEDICATION

For Jonah and Sienna.
I love you both fiercely.
I pray you understand the value and responsibility of
being a merchant of God's hope.

SPECIAL THANKS
to Matt Lockwood for your care, effort and focus in
bringing this book to life. You are a a joy to work
with. A true expert in your editing skills!

Epigraph

Era

/ˈerə/ Brit /ˈɪərə/
Noun
plural eras
: a period of time that is associated with a particular quality, event, person, etc.

PREFACE

Over the years I've learned that God associates with certain individuals in different eras to help humanity understand His generational plan and purpose. God, in His sovereign understanding, has predestined certain characters to emerge onto the stage of history to reveal the mind and nature of God.

Through Abram (who later became Abraham), one of the great patriarchs of Judaism, God shows us His ability to alter and reform the legacy of humanity by moving Abram out of his present conditions, out of the surroundings of paganism, and towards a future of covenant blessing and kingdom legacy. God promises to give Abraham descendants as many as there are stars in the sky, and through Abraham creates a new lineage of faith.

Through Moses God presents Himself as Deliverer, bringing Israel out of 400 years of slavery in Egypt with a mighty hand. Through Moses God leads His people in the establishing of the Torah, God's holy law, showing humanity the state of their sinful condition, the impact of their decisions, and the steps needed through sacrifice to walk in consecration and connection again with their Creator.

However, the Mosaic Law would only exacerbate humanity's need for a Saviour to heal the broken human condition and stir a longing in the human heart for the Messiah to redeem them.

Joshua's life represents God the Promise Fulfiller, who causes Israel to, step by step, possess their promised land, their allotted inheritance. Through Joshua, God expresses His ability to extend their lives into possessing their rightful territory, not only as a community of people but as a sovereign nation under God.

We see that Esther, in her era, was used by God to help Israel as a people understand their royal heritage. Esther also helps us understand the beauty of God's favour and His ability to impart wisdom and victory to us so that we can defeat our adversaries.

Through Nehemiah's life, we recognise God the Restorer, whose heart wept over Jerusalem's broken walls–a picture and metaphor of Israel's brokenness provoked by their historic sin and captivity. We see God, the builder of people's lives, at work, each brick built into the wall representing God's detailed steps to restore the human condition.

Then through the life of David, God reveals Himself as the Great Shepherd who guards His people, governs them, and guides His beloved sheep, Israel, through the many vicissitudes of life. Through David's life we also see God revealing His deep affection for a heart that longs after Him–and because of this God takes time and effort to pour waterfalls of grace upon David's flaws and mistakes, ensuring their intimate relationship endures eternally. Through David's life we also catch a glimpse of many other expressions of God's character: God the Warrior, God the Poet, God the Prophet, God the Righteous King, and the list goes on . . .

And now as we embark upon reading the first chapter, we will witness the transaction of God's will and purpose between David and his son Solomon. There is a radical shift of eras occurring that will ensure a continuation of legacy remains. Solomon in his kingship will go on to represent the God of peace and the God of wisdom.

1

PREPARATION FOR A NEW ERA

1 Chronicles 22:5-16

Now David said, "Solomon my son is young and inexperienced, and the house to be built for the Lord must be exceedingly magnificent, famous and glorious throughout all countries. I will now make preparation for it." So David made abundant preparations before his death.

Then he called for his son Solomon, and charged him to build a house for the Lord God of Israel. And David said to Solomon: "My son, as for me, it was in my mind to build a house to the name of the Lord my God; but the word of the Lord came to me, saying, 'You have shed much blood and have made great wars; you shall not build a house for My name, because you have shed much blood on the earth in My sight. Behold, a son shall be born to you, who shall be a man of rest; and I will give him rest from all his enemies all around. His name shall be Solomon, for I will give peace and quietness to Israel in his days. He shall build a

house for My name, and he shall be My son, and I will be
his Father; and I will establish the throne of his kingdom
over Israel forever.' Now, my son, may the Lord be with
you; and may you prosper, and build the house of the Lord
your God, as He has said to you. Only may the Lord give
you wisdom and understanding, and give you charge
concerning Israel, that you may keep the law of the Lord
your God. Then you will prosper, if you take care to fulfill
the statutes and judgments with which the Lord charged
Moses concerning Israel. Be strong and of good courage;
do not fear nor be dismayed. Indeed I have taken much
trouble to prepare for the house of the Lord one hundred
thousand talents of gold and one million talents of silver,
and bronze and iron beyond measure, for it is so
abundant. I have prepared timber and stone also, and
you may add to them. Moreover there are workmen with
you in abundance: woodsmen and stonecutters, and all
types of skillful men for every kind of work. Of gold and
silver and bronze and iron there is no limit. Arise and
begin working, and the Lord be with you."

In this passage from 1 Chronicles 22, we're catching David at the end of his kingship and Solomon at the beginning of his. The fiery baton of leadership is being passed from father to son. There's a shift occurring in the kingdom of Israel.

God takes the shift of leadership seriously because

what is at the top flows down, having the potential to bless or to curse, to build or tear down, to strengthen or weaken, to heal or hurt, to nurture or to hinder. We can learn through this passage of scripture that God denied David the opportunity to build His temple because he had too much blood on his hands. He had fought many wars and had defeated countless adversaries. David had provided an environment of peace in which his son Solomon, and all of Israel, could safely dwell. May we be sure to thank God for the warriors who have gone before us to pave the way for our freedom!

Now the Bible is very clear about the extraordinary love that God had for David: He adored him. I was confused when I read God wouldn't allow David to build the temple. The question I asked myself was, "Why? Had David offended God?" I know he'd made some pretty big mistakes, but he'd repented and had been forgiven by the Lord.

But after praying and thinking for a while God whispered something into my heart that blew my mind–He said, "Mark, ASSOCIATION MATTERS." God said, "Who and what I associate Myself with, in any given era, matters greatly to Me."

I believe God denied David the opportunity to build the temple of the Lord because David was associated with war and bloodshed, and God wanted the temple to represent peace and wisdom. And that would be the over-arching banner at that particular time in history.

The era of bloodshed had passed–God was now associating Himself with Solomon. And God was very clear about whose hands would build His temple. God wanted peace to be the flag that flew high. He wanted peace to be the sail that carried Israel into its next era.

I firmly believe that in this new era for the church, God is looking for people who can bring peace to the storm. Not a people who bring unrest and disruption but who unite hearts to usher in the sound of peace. Not a people who sit in judgement nor criticism, but a people who love fervently and exemplify a spirit of grace and understanding. There is so much unrest and volatility in the world right now that the only way people are going to see God now is through the demonstration of the complete opposite, otherwise God's Church will just blend in.

That's why when God led Israel out of Egypt. He became a cloud by day, protecting them from the heat of the desert sun. Then He became a pillar of fire by night, bringing them warmth in the evening cold. God displayed Himself as being the complete opposite to the elements they were facing so people knew it was Him that was leading them. God didn't just blend in.

That's why Jesus said, "Bless those that curse you." Because through the blessing of your enemies, the world can see and know God. That's why Jesus calmed the storm–He became the opposite of the circumstance (the storm) the disciples faced.

The world is in a battle, and I believe the last thing people want to do when they associate themself with a church is to run into yet another battle–out of the frying pan into the fire! No, I don't think that's what they want at all. Do you?

I believe God wants to show your family, your friends, and your work colleagues who He is through you by you not partnering with the climate of the culture but by showing up with the opposite heart and mind-set.

Now, Solomon represents peace and wisdom. And I believe God is calling for a Solomon era right now. You can't build in a battle–you need peace to build, stability and security to regain your footing. You can't heal in a war zone when bombs are flying and bullets are being fired, you need an environment of peace and wisdom to be healed and restored. Yet, we want to get our boxing gloves on in the current climate, have a fight, say our piece, and throw more fuel on the fire. And yes, I'm aware, there may be times when war is appropriate, and yes, there's always a time when we should speak up. But I believe with all of my heart that people are looking for a safe place, a harbour in which they can moor their life, a sanctuary where they can hear themselves think again, amid the surrounding disruption and chaos. I hope the

Church can become known for offering peace and wisdom to a confused and volatile world.

Isaiah 30:15
In returning and rest you shall be saved; In quietness and confidence shall be your strength.

John 14:27
Peace I leave with you, My peace I give to you; not as the world gives do I give to you. Let not your heart be troubled, neither let it be afraid.

Let's talk about 'preparation'. We can see that David made huge preparations for the generation that came after him. Preparations to benefit and build the next layer of God's plan and purpose with strength. We can see that, because of David, there was no shortage of material to be used for building. David had laid aside the best for God and the best for Solomon and Israel.

I'm thankful for those who think about the next generation when building the kingdom of God. I thank God for those who continue to sow and make it easier for us. King David did something that would benefit the next generation, that would benefit his son Solomon, and he focused on ensuring that his son was equipped and in a position of strength for his future reign.

FAILURE TO PREPARE

The Bible talks about a widow, in the book of 2 Kings, chapter 4, who was stressed out and anxious because her husband, a prophet, who had served under the leadership of Elisha, had died leaving her and her sons with no financial security. Her husband failed to prepare in life. Both of her sons were going to be taken into slavery to pay off their parents' debt to the creditors. Not an ideal situation to leave the next generation in! But God stepped in through Elisha the prophet and provided a pension scheme and some life insurance that would benefit the woman and her sons on this side of heaven.

We need to make sure that we are doing things this side of heaven that will benefit the next generation. If you're a dad and you're reading this, can I be so bold as to ask you a question: Have you set up any life insurance for your family? Have you set up a pension scheme that will benefit you in your old age? Are you saving or investing any money? I hope you're not offended by these questions, but I think it's so important to prepare for the future. Not only did David look after Solomon and his house financially but he also looked after the future legacy of the kingdom of God. Some people are content in looking after their own house but often the house of God remains a distant second thought. This was Nehemiah's great concern, that

Israel's walls were broken down and burned with fire. He wept about it, and then he sought to do something about it. He took it upon himself to ensure that His people's residence, their place of habitation, was restored to its rightful glory. Oh, for hearts that have a concern not just for their own house but also for the kingdom of God!

Now, I don't just want to refer to the importance of looking after the external practicalities of building and supporting the kingdom of God (although that's immensely important). I'm also mindful that we look after the spiritual qualities of our lives, looking after our soul, and specifically ensuring that we nurture our internal spiritual temple.

To me, that means looking after my mental, physical, and emotional health in a way that is unique to me. We are all different and have unique ways that feed and nurture our souls. Let's commit ourselves to finding out what makes our souls happy and do more of that.

Looking after our soul also means managing the quality of my relationships to ensure I have people around me who love me, support me, and who speak honestly and challenge me to keep stepping out so that I can grow as a person. Beyond that, I desire to continue to cultivate a heartfelt desire to build friendships and invest in God's kingdom community. That means my family and I taking the time to gather in person with the broader body of Christ. Having pioneered and pastored my own church

I know that this has been a challenge in the minds of many of God's people in recent times. Many people are not attending church on a Sunday and don't feel they are missing anything of substance for not attending. And hear my heart, I'm not so shallow as to think that attending a church gathering on a Sunday (or any day for that fact) makes you more of a Christian or gives you brownie points with God. It may give you brownie points with the pastor of the church, but not with God! However, I still think that gathering with the wider body of Christ is important as it enlarges our understanding of God because He is a multi-generational God. It also introduces us to a corporate and diverse experience with the body of Christ that you can't find in a more intimate setting.

The Covid pandemic of 2020-21 interrupted our lives to such a large degree that it reformed and restructured our patterns, rhythms, and priorities. Some of that was positive and some of that was negative. Covid also revealed what is most important to us and where our loyalties lay. I have to say that I'm still a huge advocate and believer in the gathering together of the wider body of Christ, and I (along with my family) will continue to attend, invest in and be a part of building and shaping the idea of gathering as God's great church in our local community.

In any gathering or organisational setting there has always been a unique power in coming together to share a collective experience that lets you know you are not alone, that you are a force to be reckoned with, and there will continue to be a unique power in coming together! How much more when we gather as God's great Church?

Whether on a Sunday or during the week, I pray we do not throw away the idea of gathering physically to encourage and spur one another on in our expression of faith and in following Jesus Christ.

Let me close this chapter with another look at our passage of scripture, specifically 1 Chronicles 22:6.

Then he (David) called for his son Solomon and charged him to build a house for the Lord God of Israel.

GOD CALLS BEFORE HE COMMISSIONS

I think it's significant that God used David to call Solomon into his rightful place before he charged him. The word 'charge' means to commission. That's a powerful statement and I wouldn't want us to just gloss over it. Let me repeat: God used David to call Solomon into his rightful place before he charged (commissioned) him.

Could it be that God has a rightful place for you to stand in, a place that He is calling you to stand in so that He can commission you to outwork your next era?

I have walked intimately with the Lord for over twenty-five years, and I am more than aware that God goes to great lengths to get us to where we need to be, and connected to whom we need to be doing it with. I have travelled across many waters to outwork the call of God upon my life, moving from the United Kingdom to Sydney, Australia, and back again to the United Kingdom. By the grace of God, I have had the privilege of travelling to many nations with incredible people to serve the call of God on my life. And, my friend, it was all about being positioned in the right place with the right people at the right time to outwork the call of God upon my life.

I believe this is a time when God is again calling us forward into new assignments, relational alignments, positions, and opportunities. I don't think I have ever witnessed so much movement and upheaval altogether at one time. There is so much happening around us at this time in history, on both a personal and corporate level. As I've spoken to people in my sphere of influence, I've discovered that God is continuing to use a culmination of events to move, position and station each of us for what comes next. He is busy drying things up, disrupting our normal and even bringing some things to a close that we have invested time, energy, and money in, to ensure that we move NOW, no delays! These are exciting days indeed!

I truly believe things are hotting up for a brand-new era and expression of the kingdom of God, both in word and deed. And those who have an ear to hear what the Holy Spirit is saying will be the ones whom God positions, charges, and commissions to fulfil great exploits on the frontline for His namesake. In my heart, I hear God saying, "I am calling and positioning those who will be the carriers of a new sound and a new era, and I have placed my Davids ahead of time in positions of authority to provide provision, and to call, commission and station the Solomons in their rightful place." And the Lord says, "For many have been crying out, 'Lord, send me!' However, they have been out of place, they have felt misaligned. But that has not been the case at all for My timing is not yours," says God. "I have purposely been orchestrating events to serve that which I am now ready to do. For I am a God of order, and I am a God of divine timing and strategy, and the time is now!" says the Lord.

Maybe you're saying to yourself as you're reading this, "Mark, how will I know when I've discovered my calling?"

Well, let me give you a few thoughts that I read in a book (forgive me, I can't remember the title) by John Maxwell that captured the essence of what calling is. He said (and I'm paraphrasing), "When it's your calling you won't have to chase it, it will captivate you. When it's your calling, it will match who you essentially are. Your calling will tap into your passions. Also, your calling won't just be about you, it will be about others. Your calling will be bigger than you and impossible to achieve without God's involvement. And lastly, your calling will bring a sense of purpose and fulfilment to your steps."

John's words resonated with me because we often think that calling is difficult to find and meant for 'the few', instead of having a fuller understanding and realising that calling is attached to our passion.

Always remember this, friend, (and this has helped me immensely over the years): humanity has nothing to do with manufacturing your calling. You don't pick your calling; it picks you! You know, some people think that when it comes to understanding your calling, it's like browsing around a big shop like Harvey Nichols. But that's not how calling works because the reality is you don't know yourself as God knows you.

Through the calling and charging of Solomon, we can see the wisdom and strategy of God to prearrange and prepare Solomon's life for the outworking of future events.

Friend, we have entered a new era and yesterday's mind-set can't come with you into this new place. We are in an 'era shift' a junction in the road. This is a time when God is calling and repositioning His people to be charged and commissioned into a brand-new outworking of flow and strategy.

So, association matters. I believe God is calling and commissioning individuals to show the world who He is. He is bringing those who have pre-prepared–the Davids–alongside the Solomons for a new era so that the Solomon generation is equipped to bring peace and wisdom to the storms that the world faces. Those whom God is equipping will be called and charged to do His work powerfully and effectively to extend the kingdom of God.

2

SIGHT FOR A NEW ERA

2 Kings 6:8-18

Now the king of Syria was making war against Israel; and he consulted with his servants, saying, "My camp will be in such and such a place." And the man of God sent to the king of Israel, saying, "Beware that you do not pass this place, for the Syrians are coming down there." Then the king of Israel sent someone to the place of which the man of God had told him. Thus he warned him, and he was watchful there, not just once or twice. Therefore the heart of the king of Syria was greatly troubled by this thing; and he called his servants and said to them, "Will you not show me which of us is for the king of Israel?" And one of his servants said, "None, my lord, O king; but Elisha, the prophet who is in Israel, tells the king of Israel the words that you speak in your bedroom." So he said, "Go and see where he is, that I may send and get him." And it was told him, saying, "Surely he is in Dothan." Therefore he sent horses and chariots and a great army there, and they came by night and surrounded the city. And when the servant of the man of God arose early and went out, there was an army, surrounding the city with horses and chariots. And his servant said to him, "Alas, my master! What shall we do?" So he answered, "Do not fear, for those who are with us are more than those who are with them." And Elisha prayed, and said, "Lord, I pray, open his eyes that he may see." Then the Lord opened the eyes of the young man, and he saw. And behold, the mountain was full of horses and chariots of fire all around Elisha. So when the Syrians came down to him, Elisha prayed to the Lord, and said, "Strike this people, I pray, with blindness." And He struck them with blindness according to the word of Elisha.

Before there was MI5 or the Secret Service, there was Elisha. For Israel to be victorious God had His own way of collecting secret information from Israel's enemies. God revealed the enemy's secrets to His prophet.

Elisha was an incredible man of God. He could affect people not only on a grassroots level but also on a governmental and leadership level. In fact, in terms of authority and influence, even kings were in submission to the wisdom and insight that he carried.

Oh, for a church that would impact and guide the decisions and affairs of secular government, with wisdom and discretion! Could it be that one day soon we witness a significant restoration between God's kingdom government and the way secular government conducts itself? That's a huge prayer, I know! I believe we would see the nations blessed magnificently.

In my humble opinion, as good as democracy is, it's a flawed system because it's a system that we can consistently tamper with and change. The governing laws of democracy are an unstable foundation on which to build our lives. New laws, and updates to current laws, are regularly passed, almost every week, that suit the evolving views and beliefs of an ever-changing society. This can be a benefit in some ways as it gives room for greater levels of innovation and new technological advances. It gives room for better ways of positively serving and managing our communities. And it also gives voice to those who have been overlooked, not heard, underpaid, mistreated and such. But it can also be detrimental, especially when destructive and ungodly laws are passed. The apostle Paul wrote, "A little leaven leavens the whole lump. (Galatians 5:9)" Opening the door to a minor change here and a minor change there gives room for potentially toxic ideologies to embed themselves in our society and grow. And, in many respects, this has been the case. It's no surprise that the moral fabric of our society is on a steep ever-increasing decline. It's extremely concerning. That's why we need godly people in seats of authority within our governments. We need those who have God's heart of wisdom and insight. We need those who are forward-thinking, yet able to embrace and implement the timeless truths and principles of God's Word, to ensure our society is being built upon a solid and steadfast moral foundation.

Throughout biblical history, we can read about people who were catalysts for radical change in the society they dwelt in–and God's kingdom catalysts have continued to transform society, time and time again, right up to the present day. God is seeking to work with people in playing their part to display the kingdom of God in their towns and cities.

In the passage of scripture at the start of this chapter we find Elisha is exposing the plans and strategies of the king of Syria. His prophetic gift is causing him to hear the king's secret bedroom conversations.

Now, let's play devil's advocate for a moment: just imagine the vulnerability and assault on his privacy the Syrian king must have felt.

It's most likely that you've experienced betrayal before, from those you have confided in, who have hung you out to dry and revealed private information to others. If not, then just keep on living.

But what do you do when God is the one exposing your secret plans? What do you do when God is divulging sacred information that affects the security and strength of your leadership team–and not only your leadership team but also the security of the nation that is under your authority and care? There's nowhere to run and hide when that takes place!

There was only one solution for the king of Syria, and that was to take captive or kill the one to whom these secrets were being revealed. And that man was Elisha, God's man.

The king of Syria doesn't just send a few men to capture Elisha; no, he sends a vast army–for the sake of one man! The king aimed to kill the prophetic voice.

Allow me to take a moment to talk to you about the prophetic voice.

The prophetic voice is unique all by itself, because it not only annunciates the past, and communicates the present, but it's a unique gift to us that declares the future–and that, my friend, is a very special gift indeed! Because we all want to know the future, right? Or is it just me? I believe we all have a hunger and thirst to know what happens next: like, who we will become, or what's going to take place. Some desperately want to know if they will live through the challenges that face them. Others want to know if the money will come through, or if the relationship will live or die. Some want to know if those they have been praying for will eventually change, because they've been on their knees praying for them for many years and they're at their wit's end, and they don't think that they can stay around much longer if their prayers are not heard. Others are wondering if their life will get any better.

Come on, let's be honest: the main reason we seek God is not just because we love Him, it's because He holds the future in His hands. That, my friend, is a precious gift indeed! Having foresight, all the answers and everything you need to know is true power.

He is a prophetic God. And those who honour the prophetic voice, and those who embrace it, will reap its rewards. Yes, some might say, "Mark, you have to be careful of that prophetic stuff because many in the church have abused it, to such a degree that we have become a laughingstock!"

I hear you, there's truth in that. But should that mean that we throw the baby out with the bath water? Surely not. Should that mean that we throw away the power and significance of the gift of the prophetic voice? I don't believe so, because when this gift is displayed with humility, purity, and authenticity, it is wonderful.

God's spiritual gifts truly transform lives. I've had a handful of prophetic words spoken over me over the years that have changed my life; words that have not just confirmed what was in my heart, but that have brought direction and strength to my life when I couldn't see a clear way.

However, when we use the gifts of the Spirit (and particularly the prophetic voice) for selfish ambition, to show people how great we are, we then abuse the gift. The gifts of God should only bring Glory to God.

Getting back, the king of Syria sends a vast army down to confront Elisha because he is incredibly frustrated. On this particular morning–allow me to paint the picture here–Elisha's servant Gehazi has risen early and is most likely preparing breakfast for them both. He hears a noise outside; the ground trembles, and he thinks it's an earthquake. As soon as Gehazi opens the door, he realises a vast Syrian army has surrounded Elisha's home!

At that moment Elisha and Gehazi had a choice to make: would they buy into the fact that they were surrounded and potentially defeated? Would they buy into the fact that their lives would never be the same, that they were trapped and there was no way out? Would they believe they had been overcome by their enemies, because there were thousands of military men surrounding them, and there were only two of them?

Gehazi had the kind of response that 99% of us would also have had. He was overwhelmed and shouted, "Alas, my master! What shall we do?" And that question–"What shall we do?"–is the question I want to address now. I feel it's my responsibility to offer you some insight and encouragement that will help you find sight for a new era.

The thing that stands out most to me is Elisha's response to Gehazi. It really inspired me.

Elisha said, "Do not fear, for those who are with us, are more than those who are with them." That response opens up a brave new world to us because it instantly confronts the limits and walls we create when overwhelming events have a 'face off' with us. Some would say that Elisha had lost his mind!

Let me be honest, there have been times when I have responded like Elisha, and my family have looked at me and wanted to check me into the nearest hospital, because my response seemed so ridiculous. I have had some serious persuading to do because sometimes it takes time for the situation to change. Our natural circumstances can fool us into believing that we are trapped or overwhelmed! Sometimes our natural conditions sell us the narrative that things will never change—but that is a lie. Friend, that is a fallacy. Everything is subject to change. I can honestly say, I have seen things change that I never thought was possible! More about that soon.

Elisha's response is truly remarkable, because it instantly catapults us into the realm of the impossible, into a place of total reliance upon God. His response is worth remembering when you are in an overwhelming situation because this kind of response will provoke and inspire the Lord to come to your rescue!

Elisha's response led me to my next two questions, which were, "What is Elisha seeing that his servant Gehazi isn't seeing?" and "What does Elisha have instilled in his spirit that Gehazi doesn't have?"

The answer: Elisha had vision. Elisha had his eyes fixed on something that Gehazi couldn't see, and this would be their saving grace. It would be their security.

Elisha saw into the realm of the impossible. He reached into it, latched onto an answer, a provision, a miracle in God that existed in the spiritual realm that would resolve the issue. Elisha did what God did at the beginning of creation: he spoke light into darkness, he spoke creativity into the void to produce what he needed in the now by faith! He had a vision.

Proverbs 29:18a (KJV)
Where there is no vision, the people perish.

When we can't see past our current circumstances, we will often settle with our current circumstances and give up on believing that God has something better for us around the corner.

When we lack vision, hope perishes. When we lack vision, faith diminishes. And, when we lack vision, we give room for fear to creep in instead of the answer we so desperately need.

I can understand Gehazi's response, and I can completely understand people's anxiety in these challenging times. But what we can't afford to do is let the narrative of our current circumstances govern the way we think or feel or govern the decisions we make. We must empower God's vision for our life to take centre stage.

Elisha saw something beyond the moment. He saw something that gave him entrance into another reality. He saw something that centred him and kept him anchored in hope and connected to a way through his challenge. That's why this chapter is called "Sight for a New Era" because unless we find a vision in the middle of our situation, we will sink into confusion and anxiety.

Psalm 121:1-8

I will lift up my eyes to the hills–From whence comes my help? My help comes from the Lord, Who made heaven and earth. He will not allow your foot to be moved; He who keeps you will not slumber. Behold, He who keeps Israel Shall neither slumber nor sleep. The Lord is your keeper; The Lord is your shade at your right hand. The sun shall not strike you by day, Nor the moon by night. The Lord shall preserve you from all evil; He shall preserve your soul. The Lord shall preserve your going out

and your coming in From this time forth, and even
forevermore.

The problem isn't the issue; the issue is how you see the problem. How can it be that two men who were going through the same experience saw completely different things?

The answer is that one had eyesight, and the other had God-sight. Often those two perspectives can be polar opposites!

I believe the call of the believer is to live with a sense of God-sight, to live with a sense of vision that supersedes, overwhelms, and overcomes its natural circumstances.

I believe if Elisha was standing in front of you today, he would say, "Friend, you need to see with God-sight today, as opposed to your natural sight. You need to lay hold of heaven's possibilities instead of the possibilities that your natural circumstances offer you."

With the economy of heaven, all it takes is one man's vision to usher people into a better outcome and experience.

Look at Moses, who stood in front of the Red Sea and commanded the waters to part.

Look at Gideon, who defeated an army of over one hundred thousand with just three hundred men.

Look at Samson, who defeated a thousand men with the jawbone of a donkey. And look at our Saviour, Jesus, who overcame death, hell, and the grave, and rose to life again!

Let's never lose sight of the fact that God can do the impossible for you.

Romans 8:18-19

For I consider that the sufferings of this present time are not worthy to be compared with the glory which shall be revealed in us. For the earnest expectation of the creation eagerly waits for the revealing of the sons of God.

The sons of God can only be revealed if they choose not to blend into the reality of the current moment. We need to reveal vision, peace, love, encouragement, support, and hope. We need to reveal answers, not more problems. Having vision is a powerful thing.

Jesus is the ultimate visionary, and He passed that vision on to his disciples. They were to be the continuation and legacy of His not just global but eternal vision. And now that vision has been passed to the Church of Jesus Christ and it's that vision, that reality, which is the extension of the kingdom of God, that the Church should seek to teach and declare as God's vision, narrative, and alternative for every individual.

God's will and purpose don't change because of any circumstance. The reality is the kingdom of God will work anywhere, at any time, and through anyone who chooses not to limit Him but allow Him to show up and flex His muscles.

The fact is, we are in a fight for vision. How you see is very important. You're in a 'vision fight' right now over your future, over your relationships, over your health, over your finance and over every area of your life.

Elisha's vision caused him to see something that he would not have otherwise been able to see.

Have you ever heard the story about the farmer who put his donkey into the Grand National horse race? The story goes like this. All the horse trainers said to the farmer, "He's got no chance of winning." But the farmer's response was, "I know he will not win; I just thought the company would do him good!"

The company we keep is incredibly important because it will inspire either vision or blindness, it will inspire either hope or anxiety, and it will inspire either courage or weakness.

Being around a visionary will help you catch a vision. Being around a visionary will cause you to see as they see; it will cause you to think on another level; it will cause you to leave those deadheads and find higher-quality relationships. Being around a visionary will expose you to a better way of doing things, it will help you realise you don't need to settle for second best. Being around a visionary will help you realise you don't need to fret or fuss over the circumstances because you have the ability and power through Jesus Christ to change them!

Elisha was exposed to his broader destiny by his predecessor Elijah. When his predecessor found him, Elisha was ploughing in his father's field. Now he may have been ploughing, but the fact was he wasn't a farmer. He was called to be a world-shaking, history-making prophet of God–he just didn't know it yet!

Sometimes we get stuck in the wrong narrative because we have not been exposed to a broader vision for our lives. We think we're a farmer when in fact we're a prophet of God. And sometimes we settle for being a farmer when destiny is declaring that we are something so different. Some people miss the boat because they listen to circumstances rather than listening to destiny.

Here's something to remember: when you're exposed to something greater, you'll drop something lesser. There is something great out there for you to get your hands on!

Let's look at this again: "And the mountain was full of horses and chariots of fire all around Elisha." (2 Kings 6:17)

There was fullness around Elisha. His vision equipped him with a sense of fullness; his vision equipped him with all the resources of heaven at his disposal, with security and confidence, with everything that he needed to overcome his current circumstance. There was provision available to him on an unprecedented level, he just needed to look higher, he just needed to look in the right place, and he did! I want to encourage you to look higher today!

I want you to realise that the fullness mentioned in 2 Kings 6:17 rested upon Elisha. If we remove Elisha from the story, God's fullness would remove itself from the story as well. The fullness showed up because (I believe) it mirrored or reflected what was inside Elisha's heart! God gives His fullness to people who carry a heart and passion for His vision and Elisha was a prophet of God who carried a heart and passion for heaven's vision for that time and that hour.

And I want you to realise, my friend, that it's your time and your hour. You are to be a carrier of God's vision, the potential carrier of your family's Sight for a New Era. You are the potential carrier for your community's Sight for a New Era, for your town, your city, and the nation's Sight for a New Era.

What will you choose to see? What will you choose to reach for when you face insurmountable odds? How will you choose to reach out to God when you're staring impossibilities in the face? How will you respond? How will you react? Will you crumble in a heap, or will you choose to reach to God for Sight for a New Era?

Your choice will determine the narrative and reality you give life to. Choose well, my friend. Choose well.

3
POSITIONED FOR A NEW ERA

1 Samuel 30:1-8

Now it happened, when David and his men came to Ziklag, on the third day, that the Amalekites had invaded the South and Ziklag, attacked Ziklag and burned it with fire, and had taken captive the women and those who were there, from small to great; they did not kill anyone, but carried them away and went their way. So David and his men came to the city, and there it was, burned with fire; and their wives, their sons, and their daughters had been taken captive. Then David and the people who were with him lifted up their voices and wept, until they had no more power to weep. And David's two wives, Ahinoam the Jezreelitess, and Abigail the widow of Nabal the Carmelite, had been taken captive. Now David was greatly distressed, for the people spoke of stoning him, because the soul of all the people was grieved, every man for his sons and his daughters. But David strengthened himself in the Lord his God. Then David said to Abiathar

*the priest, Ahimelech's son, "Please bring the ephod here
to me." And Abiathar brought the ephod to David. So
David inquired of the Lord, saying, "Shall I pursue this
troop? Shall I overtake them?"*

*And He answered him, "Pursue, for you shall surely
overtake them and without fail recover all."*

David's journey of being positioned by God was not
without challenge and, dare I say it, not without
pain. There were many battles, many betrayals and
rejections that took place in David's life to propel him
into a place of leadership influence and kingdom authority.

Many people seek the path of least resistance. What
I've learned over the last twenty-six years of being a
believer, and the last twenty-something years I've been
in full-time ministry, is that if you're seeking to do anything
great for God, you need to get used to challenge and
disappointment.

You need to stomach high levels of resistance and
conflict because there will be many opposing forces and
opinions that will seek to take you off course. It's then
that you need to train yourself to lean hard on God; it's
then that you need to train yourself to stay in peace and
remember the thing that God has called you to achieve.

On our way towards being positioned by God, there

will be seasons of preparation, birthed in complex experiences. But it's in those experiences that God forms the character of His Son within you.

There are very few, if any, overnight success stories in the kingdom of God. We can learn from the Bible that God sometimes took decades to prepare and position people for maximum impact and effect. I've learned that God deliberately takes his time to introduce us to certain experiences, to certain people and places who will each play a part in preparing you for the position that God has pre-designed and pre-arranged for you to walk in so that by the time you get there, you'll be ready! You'll be ready like David who, by the time he got to fight Goliath, had prepared by fighting the lion and the bear.

Living in real-time often forbids us the luxury of understanding where, when and how God will position us for maximum impact. Usually, we only understand God's plan and purpose in hindsight. The Bible says, "All the days ordained for me were written in His book before one ever came to be." (Psalm 139:16)

God knows exactly what He's doing, even when we don't!

I've called this chapter 'Positioned for a New Era' because I believe the landscape of God's Church is radically changing, and with that change is coming a lot of readjustment and repositioning. I'm not just talking about physical readjustment and repositioning, but also mental, spiritual, and emotional repositioning. This is something that I believe is happening quickly across the world.

The challenges and complexities of this moment in history in which we find ourselves are quickly revealing hearts and exposing belief systems and ideologies. I think that's a very exciting prospect because those who have possibly been in a cloud of confusion regarding the direction of their life, or those who have been unclear about where people stand, are beginning to see the picture made plain.

I believe God is sifting hearts on a global level; I believe God is revealing to us what we care about, what we value the most and what we want to dedicate the rest of our lives to over the long term.

A new era has dawned upon us, and God has been busy re-shuffling the deck and repositioning His players. And He's not doing this behind the scenes, He's doing this in front of our eyes, out in the open. This is not a private thing that the Lord is doing, but a public transformation of the Church.

I wanted to lift the life of David to you because I think David's positioning by God was a very swift and public one. I'm not referring to David's years of preparation time here, I am talking about the culmination of events that led to positioning David into a seat of influence that would impact his generation and the generations thereafter. It looked like it happened almost overnight. When God moves in your life, He will make things happen in a day that would take you a decade to form or create through your own strength!

In the passage of scripture, we read at the beginning of this chapter, David has returned home to Ziklag with his six hundred men and finds the town burned to the ground. The whole place has gone up in smoke! His two wives and children, and the wives and children of the men who fight with him, have been abducted and carried away by the Amalekites, an enemy army. And as if that's not bad enough, David's men are threatening to kill him because they believe David has led them into this disaster. Ah, the joys of leadership! Not a very nice day at the office for David.

I'm always fascinated with the details the Bible gives us concerning people's lives and how God moved to get them to where they needed to be. Let me give you a bit of context here because I want you to understand how God positions us for something new.

GOD IS A GOD OF DETAIL

To remind you, the town where David and his family have been staying, that's now a pile of ashes, is called Ziklag. It was a city given to David as a gift by King Achish.

1 Samuel 27:3-6

So David dwelt with Achish at Gath, he and his men, each man with his household, and David with his two wives, Ahinoam the Jezreelitess, and Abigail the Carmelitess, Nabal's widow. And it was told Saul that David had fled to Gath; so he sought him no more.

Then David said to Achish, "If I have now found favor in your eyes, let them give me a place in some town in the country, that I may dwell there. For why should your servant dwell in the royal city with you?" So Achish gave him Ziklag that day. Therefore Ziklag has belonged to the kings of Judah to this day."

Achish was the king of Gath, and Gath was one of the Philistine regions. That might not mean much to you, but the Philistines were arch-enemies of Israel. Israel is where David is from! Israel was being ruled over by David's father-in-law, King Saul, who had been chasing David for many years. David had escaped from King Saul and defected from Israel to hide himself from the madness of his father-in-law who, because of his bitter envy and jealousy of David, sought to kill him. David thought to himself, "Well, what better place to hide than in enemy territory?" David heads to Gath, a Philistine town, and is given the city of Ziklag, and while there he fights on behalf of the Philistines, winning many battles.

When Ziklag is being burned with fire, the Philistine army are going out to war against Israel, and that is very significant, because this was a battle that David would be involved in, but he would fight on behalf of the Philistines and not his own people, Israel. He would effectively be fighting against his own people and the nation that he would soon become king over and rule. Not only that, but he would also be fighting against his father-in-law King Saul, and his brother-in-law Jonathan, his beloved friend.

God was very shrewd and turned the hearts of some of the Philistine leaders against David, not letting him go out and battle against Israel, or against Saul and Jonathan, his family. God ensured that would not happen because God was busy preparing to position David for future events!

I say all that to encourage someone who feels like you've defected from Plan A, and now you're having to deviate to fulfil a role that doesn't really fit you. You may be in a job, a relational circle, or a situation that doesn't fit you. It's not your promised land. And because of the circumstances that you find yourself in, you're having to adapt and make choices you wouldn't normally make, for you and for the sake of your family.

I just want to encourage you by saying that God is in this, and He is with you. You may feel you're taking steps away from your calling, but I want to tell you that you're taking steps towards it.

Watch what happens to David...

Ziklag is burnt to the ground, and David's men want to kill him. What does David do? His response is to seek the Lord. God gives him clear direction regarding his next move. God says, "Pursue the enemy, for you shall surely overtake them, and without fail, recover all." (1 Samuel 30:8)

After David has sought the Lord, he persuades most of his men to follow him in winning back their families. And they do just that!

Now, here's what I want you to get: while that's happening, while David is winning back his family, an era is ending on a separate battlefield. While David is pouring his energy and passion into fighting for his family over here, God is busy fighting for him over there. Here comes the shift of position for a new era.

King Saul, his son Jonathan, and two other sons, lost their lives that day, killed in a bloody and brutal way by the Philistines. The Philistines make a public spectacle of Saul, cutting his body into pieces and sending them across the region as a memento of their victory over Israel! But by God's Grace, David is removed and hidden from seeing any of this, from being implicated in any of these events.

In my opinion, Jonathan should not have been on the same battlefield as his father Saul that day, he should've been on the battlefield next to David! Jonathan had pledged his undying love and support for David over many years, but he had failed to separate from his father, Saul. He had failed to reposition himself alongside his most esteemed friend, David. Maybe Jonathan's reason for not separating from his father was because he was enjoying the benefits of being a king's son, rather than deciding to 'rough it' alongside David. However, roughing it would've been a much better option because his life would have been saved for the long term by putting up with short-term discomfort! Some people stay where they are and with whom they are with because they are not willing to be inconvenienced. Yet their unwillingness to be inconvenienced can damage their future blessing and physical, emotional, and spiritual prosperity!

David was, of course, next in line for the throne, but it had been many years since he had been anointed to be Israel's next King by the prophet Samuel. Samuel was long dead and gone, and I'm sure even David wondered, "How on earth is this ever going to take place?" Maybe he had given up on the whole idea, who knows? But within a day, everything changed. A radical shift of events took place and God positioned David for his future reign.

After Saul and his sons were killed, David gets a knock

at his door–a man turns up with a crown in his hands. It's the crown of kingship that Saul had worn. That man bringing the crown thinks he's doing David a favour by bearing the devastating news that Saul had been slain with his sons on a battlefield. But he quickly finds out how presumptuous he has been. When he explains to David that he was implicated in Saul's death, David immediately executes him! David had had several opportunities in the past to take Saul's life, but he would never do it because he would not touch God's anointed. David had a healthy fear of God.

David is left standing there with the crown of kingship in his hands, and the revelation that an era has passed would immediately dawn upon him. He laments over the passing of Saul and Jonathan, capturing it in a Psalm, called 'The Song of the Bow', now embedded in biblical history forever.

2 Samuel 1:23-27
"Saul and Jonathan were beloved and pleasant in their lives,
And in their death they were not divided;
They were swifter than eagles,
They were stronger than lions.
"O daughters of Israel, weep over Saul,
Who clothed you in scarlet, with luxury;
Who put ornaments of gold on your apparel.

"How the mighty have fallen in the midst of the battle!
Jonathan was slain in your high places.
I am distressed for you, my brother Jonathan;
You have been very pleasant to me;
Your love to me was wonderful,
Surpassing the love of women.
"How the mighty have fallen,
And the weapons of war perished!"

Isn't it amazing how David didn't gloat over his enemies? He had every reason to gloat, considering his father-in-law had hunted him down for his very life for many years. But he honoured Saul and Jonathan in their deaths. That takes a big person!

On the darkest of days in David's life, a day where he is mourning the loss of Saul and Jonathan, a day where he's mourning the passing of an era, the crown of kingship is passed to him, and things radically change in his life.

David moves up to Judah and settles in a place called Hebron, and there he is anointed and positioned as the king of Judah for seven years. No more would he dwell in the wilderness, in enemy territory with six hundred men, and no more would he be chased down for his very life. Now he would move into a new era, where hundreds of thousands of talented and skilled men would gather around him.

I once heard a great man of God say that "Success never feels like success because of the pain and heartache it took you to get you there." I believe that. Because kingdom success never looks like the world's success. Kingdom success is all about service unto God and taking responsibility. The anointing that rested upon David's life wasn't about giving people goosebumps, it was about being effective and outworking the will of God powerfully to further and extend the kingdom of God.

In the middle of a mess, God did something astounding in David's life that would affect the next forty years of his life! Not only that, but it would also affect the generations to come.

I pray you would be mindful today that God is working on your behalf in a powerful, profound, and significant way. There is an era shift at hand, I firmly believe it; God is positioning you for what comes next!

Let's finish this chapter by reading this:

2 Samuel 2:1-4
"It happened after this that David inquired of the Lord, saying, "Shall I go up to any of the cities of Judah?" And the Lord said to him, "Go up." David said, "Where shall I go up?" And He said, "To Hebron." So David went up there, and his two wives also, Ahinoam the Jezreelitess, and Abigail the widow of Nabal the Carmelite. And David

brought up the men who were with him, every man with his household. So they dwelt in the cities of Hebron. Then the men of Judah came, and there they anointed David king over the house of Judah. And they told David, saying, "The men of Jabesh Gilead were the ones who buried Saul."

4
LIMPING INTO A NEW ERA

Genesis 32:24-32

Then Jacob was left alone; and a Man wrestled with him until the breaking of day. Now when He saw that He did not prevail against him, He touched the socket of his hip; and the socket of Jacob's hip was out of joint as He wrestled with him. And He said, "Let Me go, for the day breaks." But he said, "I will not let You go unless You bless me!" So He said to him, "What is your name?" He said, "Jacob." And He said, "Your name shall no longer be called Jacob, but Israel; for you have struggled with God and with men, and have prevailed." Then Jacob asked, saying, "Tell me Your name, I pray." And He said, "Why is it that you ask about My name?" And He blessed him there. So Jacob called the name of the place Peniel: "For I have seen God face to face, and my life is preserved." Just as he crossed over Penuel the sun rose on him, and he limped on his hip. Therefore to this day the children of Israel do not eat the muscle that shrank, which is on the

*hip socket, because He touched the socket of Jacob's hip in
the muscle that shrank.*

At the heart of the human experience is a desire to
know who we are and what we were born for.
Embedded within the core of our being is a yearning and
predisposition to find out why we've been given the
opportunity of living life.

The Bible teaches us we are predestined to be here.
You are not an accident. No matter what your background
is, or the circumstances that surrounded your arrival,
you are part of a divinely orchestrated plan. God had a
prearranged purpose for your life before you even showed
up as an idea in your mother's and father's mind. Even
before your parents saw your heartbeat on a screen at
the hospital, God knew you and He knew exactly when
to open the curtains on the stage of history so that you
could play your part in His eternal, unfolding drama.

God's purpose for our life is often shrouded in mystery.
The Bible says, "We see in a mirror, dimly" (1 Corinthians
13:12), giving us an understanding that we struggle to
see our purpose with complete clarity. Although there
are those brief light bulb moments, those epiphanies,
where we see and hear things that bring long-term
direction to our lives, those moments may not happen
very often. But even one of them can steer the ship of

our life towards our destination, steering us away from damaging reefs and undercurrents that seek to thwart the plan of God for our life.

When I read about the life of Jacob, I read about someone who was on a desperate search to find his identity. The Bible reveals to us, that he had some kind of unconscious struggle to find his destiny. Even in his mother's womb, he latched onto his twin brother Esau's heel to race him to the winner's post for the birthright that would rest upon the life of the firstborn son. Jacob was therefore named 'supplanter' or 'deceiver,' because even at his birth he sought to move his brother out of the way and make a way for himself, no matter the cost.

Although Jacob had been born second and had therefore missed out on being a recipient of the birthright, he seemed to live with much more of a passion and desire for the birthright than his brother Esau. Maybe Esau lived with a sense of entitlement that Jacob didn't have the luxury of living with. But Jacob seemed to live with a sense of intensity and focus on the birthright that Esau lacked.

I want to call this 'older sibling syndrome'. It's the syndrome that can exist in an overbearing, domineering, older sibling who lives with a sense of entitlement that belittles the younger. However, with that sense of entitlement, there eventually comes a fall, especially when opportunities are passed to those who have the right heart and attitude.

We can see this take place in the life of a young David, who was overlooked and belittled by his older brothers, particularly Eliab. Yet, God had his eye on David. God loved his heart and David was anointed to be Israel's future King.

Jacob and Esau were very different guys. Jacob was a mild-mannered, stay-at-home-and-cook kind of guy, and Esau was the hunter-gatherer, go-out-and-kill-it kind of guy. Their father Isaac preferred Esau, because of his hunter-gatherer nature and, of course, Esau was the first-born son, so I expect Isaac viewed him with a sense of legacy and continuum.

But let me say this: when God lays His hand on you for destiny and decides that it's you He wants to raise up, it doesn't matter who you are, or what postcode you're from, and it doesn't matter that you're perceived to be second best in the eyes of those closest to you. If God has destined you for greatness, He will bypass protocol to get the job done! He will move everything around you to favour, the calling He has placed upon your life.

Jacob had a supernatural desire and passion built within him to get his hands on Esau's birthright. Jacob was hungry for the blessing of God to manifest in his life. There was something within him that pushed him and provoked him, that propelled him to mess with the order.

Genesis 25:29-34

Now Jacob cooked a stew; and Esau came in from the field, and he was weary. And Esau said to Jacob, "Please feed me with that same red stew, for I am weary." Therefore his name was called Edom. But Jacob said, "Sell me your birthright as of this day." And Esau said, "Look, I am about to die; so what is this birthright to me?" Then Jacob said, "Swear to me as of this day." So he swore to him, and sold his birthright to Jacob. And Jacob gave Esau bread and stew of lentils; then he ate and drank, arose, and went his way. Thus Esau despised his birthright.

Can you believe it? Esau cared more about food than his birthright! He cared more about the current moment he was in than his broader destiny and future inheritance. Either it was that, or Jacob was an unusually talented chef! Put it this way: Jacob must have been able to cook a mean stew for Esau to consider giving up his birthright! This must've been Michelin-star quality dining!

When it was time for their father, Isaac, to physically pass on the birthright in a family gathering, Jacob's mother Rebekah devised a plan to manufacture events to ensure Jacob would become the beneficiary of Isaac's blessing and not Esau. God had spoken to Rebekah while her two sons were being carried in her womb, saying that the older brother would serve the younger and that the firstborn would serve the second-born.

Genesis 25:22-23

But the children struggled together within her; and she said, "If all is well, why am I like this?" So she went to inquire of the Lord. And the Lord said to her: "Two nations are in your womb, Two peoples shall be separated from your body; One people shall be stronger than the other, And the older shall serve the younger."

So even before their birth, the prophetic word of God was being made flesh and was dividing the twins. The word of God has a way of transforming circumstances to suit itself. God has a plan, and it will happen, no matter the cost because He is God, and beside Him there is no other!

Because of the word that God had spoken to Rebekah, she felt it necessary to force events to cause Jacob to receive the promise of the birthright. She'd overheard her husband Isaac speaking to Esau, saying, "I am close to death, and it's now time for me to pass on to you your birthright. Please take your weapons, your quiver and your bow, and go out and hunt game for me. And make me savoury food, such as I love, Bring it to me that I may eat, that my soul may bless you before I die." (Genesis 27:2-4)

This is quite a critical moment in Isaac's life. Here is

a window of opportunity where Isaac is ready to pass on the birthright and blessing that would affect the lineage of God's people. This is BIG news!

But this big news will not be shouted from the rooftops, it will not be televised on the News. This big news will not be on the cover of a magazine, no! Usually, when God does something big, and transformative in your life, it will be packaged amid very normal and mundane circumstances. Anything God does in our life will arrive as a seed–but in that seed is incredible potential.

I pray you will become more aware of the small, seemingly insignificant things that occur in your life because their smallness does not deny the power of a seed's ability to completely transform your life.

Rebekah had overheard Isaac's conversation with Esau and was now ready to orchestrate events in Jacob's favour to ensure the birthright was passed to him. Whether this was God's original intention, I'm not sure. God has a thousand ways to bless you. Nonetheless, He permitted Rebekah to orchestrate events to ensure the blessing was bequeathed to Jacob.

God is, of course, the God who knows the end from the beginning, and He will permit certain events to take place to ensure His plan comes to pass. The truth of the matter is, Rebekah was a deceiver too. She was a supplanter herself; it ran in the family.

Isn't it amazing how sin can perpetuate and strengthen itself in each successive generation that follows? Often, we end up dealing with the fruit our children produce, failing to realise the root of the tree is within us.

So, while Esau was out hunting game for his father, Rebekah dresses Jacob up like his brother and pushes him in front of his father to deceive him into passing on the birthright.

Isaac was very old, and his eyesight was weak. Therefore, he mistakenly passes on an irreversible blessing to Jacob, thinking it was Esau. Isaac asks Jacob, "Who are you, my son?" And Jacob says, "I am Esau." And from the act of deception, a series of events unfold leading to Jacob running for his life from his brother's hot temper, who later plots to kill him!

Jacob was warned by his mother that Esau wanted to kill him. Jacob is sent away by his father Isaac, and so Jacob goes to live with his uncle Laban, his mother's brother.

Jacob moves away from his family with a sense of stolen identity. Have you ever stolen something and lived with a sense of guilt because of what you've taken? It's one thing to steal an item from a shop, but what do you do when you steal someone else's identity?

I think, deep within Jacob, was a sense of not knowing who he was. I've realised that God's validation for our lives can be received when we're willing to be honest with ourselves, when we are ready to be open and vulnerable about who we are and what we've done. Some people never find out who they truly are because they're on the run inside themselves. They're living a lie and they're immersed in shame; they're locked up in a prison cell made by their own mistakes and they don't know how to escape, hiding from who they truly are because of what they've done!

Jacob runs away from his past into his future with a seed of deception planted within him, and that seed of deception would reproduce itself wherever he went until it was dealt with. He finds favour with his uncle Laban, in the land of Padan Aram, and falls in love with Laban's daughter, Rachel. Then, for his wages, he works for seven years for Rachel's hand in marriage. She must've been quite something to agree to work for seven years for her hand in marriage, well worth waiting for!

Jacob loved Rachel dearly, but after working for seven years Laban deceives Jacob and gave him his eldest daughter Leah, who apparently wasn't so attractive. Jacob did not love Leah.

I think we can see a problem reproducing itself here, can we not? The seed of deception is reproducing itself in Jacob's circumstances. But because of Jacob's great love for Rachel, he worked another seven years for her hand in marriage. Eventually, Laban fulfilled his word and gave his daughter Rachel to Jacob to be his wife.

Jacob would stay and serve Laban for around twenty years. God prospered Jacob because of Isaac's birthright blessing that rested upon him. God gave Jacob twelve sons and one daughter, and he became incredibly wealthy. But he still didn't know who he truly was because he was still living with a sense of stolen identity.

Something was deeply unresolved within Jacob. He longed to return home to his family because there was unfinished business to deal with. Unfinished business can stay with you all your life... It will keep you up at night. It will gnaw at your soul. It will climb into bed with you, and in some cases, put you on prescription medication. It will turn you into a recluse.

And so, Jacob packs up all of his things and begins the long and complex journey of separating from his father-in-law, Laban, taking his wives, children, cattle and belongings, and they travel on foot back home to Gerar, which is a distance of about one hundred and forty-four miles.

On the road home, when everyone is exhausted, Jacob receives news from his messengers, that his brother Esau is coming out to meet him with four hundred men. Fear is struck into the heart of Jacob; the last time he saw his brother, Esau wanted to kill him for stealing the birthright.

Jacob separates his family and cattle and sends half of his belongings ahead of him as a gift to Esau, in the hopes his brother spares, his life and the lives of his family. It's in that place of fear, concern, and uncertainty that Jacob is left alone with God. It's in that place that a wrestle for Jacob's true identity would take place, that Jacob would finally find out who he truly was, and he would lay hold of something that belonged solely to him.

I think it's significant that Esau is on his way to meet him, the brother whom Jacob had deceived. It's like God was taking the opportunity to ensure that by the time the brothers meet face-to-face again, Jacob is not whom he used to be. God meets Jacob in a powerful way.

Genesis 32:24-28

Then Jacob was left alone; and a Man wrestled with him until the breaking of day. Now when He saw that He did not prevail against him, He touched the socket of his hip; and the socket of Jacob's hip was out of joint as He wrestled with him. And He said, "Let Me go, for the day breaks." But he said, "I will not let You go unless You bless me!" So He said to him, "What is your name?" He said, "Jacob." And He said, "Your name shall no longer be called Jacob, but Israel; for you have struggled with God and with men, and have prevailed."

I think it's worthy of attention that God asks Jacob, "What is your name?" His father Isaac had asked Jacob the same question many years ago, and Jacob had lied and said he was Esau. But now he has an opportunity to redeem himself. Names carry meaning, particularly in the cultures of that time. They gave people an understanding of who you were, and the circumstances that surrounded your birth.

So, in this moment of encounter, God takes the opportunity to change his name, from Jacob to Israel, from deceiver to Prince with God. I believe a name change is going on right now. God is bringing clarity and definition to people's lives so they know who they are, so they know whom to trust, and so they know which direction to move in next.

PROPHETIC WORD

"You've been in a wrestle for your identity, and you can't come into this next level as the old you." And God says, "I'm causing a transformation to take place on the inside of you. And the way you have historically seen yourself and the way others have seen you is about to change." For God says, "I am dealing with the root cause of those things that have hindered you from entering into the fullness of whom I've called you to be. A name change is about to occur. There is a shift of identity taking place." And God says, "This new

era that you are entering will not be based on who you were, but on who you are becoming. I'm breaking the past of you and I'm bringing you into the fullness of your destiny. The past will no longer define you, and what hindered you, will hinder you no more," says the Lord.

Lastly, I want you to notice that God gave Jacob a limp by shrinking the muscle in his hip. I called this chapter, 'Limping into a New Era,' because I firmly believe, God is going to give you, a spiritual limp.

PROPHETIC WORD

God says, "I'm going to cause things to shrink in your life that you've historically relied upon to give you muscle for your momentum. I'm going to cause those things to shrink and atrophy in your life. I'm going to cause them to ebb away. Things that you thought you needed... people that you thought you needed. The circumstances are changing, and the muscle is shrinking, and I'm causing things to diminish and weaken that you thought you needed to propel you further." And God says, "I'm changing your name today, from supplanter to Israel, from deceiver to Prince with God. For you cannot go into this next era as Jacob, and you cannot go into this next dimension, unless I change your name, and change your nature. Nor, can you live in the revelation of yesterday, nor carry the baggage of yesterday. It's time, for Israel to come forth! It's time, for a new sound, and a new mindset to be birthed!" For God says, "I am removing those who have held you in a lesser version of whom I've called you to be. And I'm now bringing into your orbit, those who will see you in the light of, the new you." And the Lord says, "So as I prove My promise to you, you shall walk with a spiritual limp, and everyone will know, that you have wrestled with God, and God won. And this limp will not hinder your momentum, but it will strengthen it. This limp will not slow the process, but it will hasten it! This limp will not be to your detriment but to your advantage. It will not work against you, but work for you. For you shall limp into a new era! And you will walk as a Prince with God." And God says, "For you will sense new freedom and authority, and you will begin to see new things happen, and new things will be birthed, that will bless your children and your children's children. So, rejoice! For I the Lord will cause you to limp into this new era!" says the Lord.

The reality is, there's only so far that we can go in our own strength, or by self-creation. To reach our ultimate destination, we're going to have to get there with the validation of God, not with the validation of our own idea, or with the validation of a stolen identity. Jacob's validation would be based on the embracing of his true identity, in God.

Friend, I believe, that what worked for you in the last era, will not necessarily work for you in this next era. I believe that to reach the pinnacle of your destiny, you need a name change–you need a spiritual limp.

5

LEAPING INTO A NEW ERA

Luke 1:39-45

Now Mary arose in those days and went into the hill country with haste, to a city of Judah, and entered the house of Zacharias and greeted Elizabeth. And it happened, when Elizabeth heard the greeting of Mary, that the babe leaped in her womb; and Elizabeth was filled with the Holy Spirit. Then she spoke out with a loud voice and said, "Blessed are you among women, and blessed is the fruit of your womb! But why is this granted to me, that the mother of my Lord should come to me? For indeed, as soon as the voice of your greeting sounded in my ears, the babe leaped in my womb for joy. Blessed is she who believed, for there will be a fulfillment of those things which were told her from the Lord."

In the last chapter, I wrote about limping into a New Era. We focused on the life of Jacob, who had his identity changed from supplanter or deceiver to Israel, Prince with God. Jacob was the recipient of his father, Isaac's birthright, but because of the act of deception that was responsible for stealing the birthright, the Lord wrestled with Jacob, in changing not only his name but his nature, and giving him a limp would be the sign that he had wrestled with God and God had won!

In this chapter, I want to talk to you about leaping into a New Era, and that might sound like a contradiction. You might ask, "How can we go from limping to leaping?" Well, all shall be made plain because I believe both actions (limping and leaping) are supernatural responses to the Holy Spirit's calling and destiny upon our life for this new era. Limping refers to the awakening of identity, but leaping refers to the confirmation and outworking, of your identity.

As we peer into this story and begin to make ourselves familiar with the circumstances that contribute to it, we find ourselves entering a supernatural rhythm of the Holy Spirit that rests upon the lives of both Mary and Elizabeth, two incredible matriarchs of biblical history.

The train has just left the station, as it were, and Mary is making haste to her cousin Elizabeth's house to find a place of refuge, safety and understanding. For what she has conceived within her womb is something that very few will understand. What God is doing in her life can only be described as supernatural and unusual.

Before her arrival at Elizabeth's home, Mary has been visited by the angel Gabriel, who has announced to her, "Do not be afraid Mary, for you have found favour with God. And, behold, you will conceive in your womb and bring forth a Son and shall call His name Jesus. He will be great and will be called the Son of the Highest, and the Lord will give Him the throne of His father David. And he will reign over the house of Jacob forever and of His kingdom, there shall be no end. The Holy Spirit will come upon you and the power of the Most High will overshadow you, therefore, also, that Holy One who is to be born will be called the Son of God." (Luke 1:30-35)

Mary was going to be carrying something so precious; more precious than anything that has ever been carried: the consolation of Israel, the Messiah. Generations of women had no doubt prayed that they would be the ones to carry the Messiah. Oh, what a privilege, and what an honour!

Let me ask you a question: have you ever carried something incredibly expensive? It makes you walk differently, doesn't it? It makes you walk with a different level of awareness and care. It will change your behaviour and will intensify your sense of protectiveness.

Have you ever had the privilege of driving something incredibly expensive? You hold the wheel with both hands and you're oversensitive and mindful of your surroundings because you don't want to dent or damage that thing!

Mary is carrying something priceless, expensive, and unusual. She comes to the right house because Elizabeth's circumstances are anything but normal as well. She too is carrying a child, and the circumstances which surround her child's conception are also out of the box!

PROPHETIC WORD

I believe God is getting ready to break the box in this season! And I heard the Lord say, "Yes, I'm getting ready to break the box! I'm changing the pattern and I'm changing the order, and I'm taking my people into a divine rhythm that is born of My Spirit." And the Lord says, "I'm planting new things down inside the womb of your consciousness on this day, that will be birthed as a catalyst for this new era. And what I'm birthing will be out of the ordinary and it shall be unusual. And everyone will know that it is of Me, for it shall kick in the womb of your spirit, and it shall make you uncomfortable, for I am planting new things on the inside of you, even on this day, and in this very hour," says the Lord.

The same angel, Gabriel, visited Elizabeth's husband, Zacharias, only six months before Mary's arrival, and announced that he and his wife Elizabeth would conceive a child in their old age. That child was John the Baptist, the cousin of Jesus.

During the angelic visitation, Zacharias failed to believe at first and was struck dumb by the angel. Now, as we enter this moment in the lives of Mary and Elizabeth, Zacharias is still under the effect of not being able to speak or utter a word. He is, in fact, mute.

PROPHETIC WORD

And the Lord says, "I'm going to shut their mouth! Yes, I'm going to shut every mouth that is against you, and it shall not hinder you nor come near your dwelling. It shall be like water off a duck's back" says God. And the Lord says, "You shall not be swayed to the left nor the right. I'm going to cause a spirit of joy to rise on the inside of you, for I shall justify you and raise you up to be a sign, that I am able to do what I have said, that I am able to do what I have promised." And the Lord says, "So do not be dismayed by the voices and opinions that oppose you. For they shall be mute and unable to disturb what I'm doing through you in this season and at this time. For I'm getting ready to dumbfound even you and those around you, because I am birthing a new era! Yes, the birthright is upon you, and the birthright is your inheritance, and the birthright will straighten the path and make a way for plain sight." For the Lord says, "This new era will be the breeding ground for greatness. This new era will be the breeding ground for the next generation of sons and daughters that I am raising up," says God. "So go forth in My strength and My power and do not be afraid, for I the Lord have gone before you to prepare the way," says God.

God has visited the lives of Mary, Zacharias, and Elizabeth. Something magnificent was taking place. In the scripture that we read earlier, we have two women going through very similar circumstances, meeting up with one another and something truly unique is happening before very eyes.

Both women are the recipients of a new era that is just about to dawn upon their lives, upon their community, and upon the nation of Israel. And not only the nation of Israel—what they both carry will have an impact on the world and all that follows thereafter.

This is BIG!

As I mentioned in the previous chapter regarding the encounter between Isaac and Jacob and the passing on of the birthright, the birthright that Isaac handed to Jacob didn't look big at the time, it was a simple prophetic blessing. But the magnitude of 'blessing' contained within it was the most profound and significant thing that was ever to be handed down to any individual to date. Isaac was handing to Jacob the blessing and birthright through which Christ would come.

I think that often, because of the mundane and quite beige circumstances that often surround us as recipients of what God is seeking to do, we fail to realise how precious what we are being handed, or what we are carrying, truly is. Often what gets passed on to us is not fully understood, honoured, or recognised, particularly by those around us.

PROPHETIC WORD

But the Lord wants to say today, "The circumstances do not deny the significance of what I've given you to carry. The circumstances do not diminish the power and authenticity of what I have placed down on the inside of you. The lack of support, encouragement, and celebration that you have experienced does not downgrade the quality and substance of my promise." For the Lord says, "I'm getting ready to multiply all that I placed on the inside of you. And you shall prosper and go forth in leaps and bounds. You should go forth with a supernatural momentum. For I'm breathing new breath into your spirit as of this day. I am bringing a great refreshing so you'll be able to stand on your own two feet and leap into your destiny. This is a good day, and this is a good time. Nothing has changed in Me towards you. And My desire to bless and prosper you is still as strong and as clear as it has ever been. Yes, My favour towards you has not wavered nor weakened. For it is impossible for Me to lie. My Word is good. My Word is truth. My Bond is unshakable! So get ready, for the time is here, and the time is now in the time is even at the door," says the Lord.

We need to recognise that Mary and Elizabeth, carried two eras within them. Any Bible scholar will know that Jesus Christ fulfilled the law of Moses, down to every last detail. Jesus was the perfect sacrifice for there was no sin in Him. He would be responsible for birthing us into a new era. And that new era was, of course, the dispensation of grace. For the law came through Moses, but grace and truth came through Jesus Christ.

The era of law that Jesus the Messiah and John the Baptist were born into would soon come to an end. John the Baptist would prophetically declare the dawning of a new era for John's message was, "Behold the Son of God, who taketh away the sins of the world." Or in other words (and allow me to paraphrase here), "Behold, the Son of God who will fulfil the law, the old era, and birth us into a new era, the dispensation of grace!"

Mary and Elizabeth's destinies are connected to

greatness and purpose. Their destinies are woven together by God, one unlocking the next, one honouring the next. There would be no dishonour between John the Baptist and Jesus Christ. They both held each other in the highest esteem. They both realised they existed to serve one another in a continuum. One era joined to the next.

Honour is a powerful thing. It's a much-needed quality in the Body of Christ. I believe we need to be incredibly careful in speaking well of one another and appreciating all that we carry from one era to the next. When there's an era shift, I find that both eras can often throw stones at one another rather than honouring one another.

You can't be transformational until you've been traditional. Let me explain that.

You can't change something that you first haven't been attached to. You can't make something better that you haven't first taken the time to understand. You'll notice in Christ's journey that He had to live in and fulfil the era of law before He birthed us into a new era. In other words, Jesus would honour the era of law before He ushered us into the era of grace.

Some come in like a bull in a china shop who try to change something, failing to bring honour where honour is due. They come in and run roughshod, treading over people who have spent their lives building an era of ministry, or building an era of business, an era of family, or an era of community. They fail to honour the blood, sweat, and tears of the predecessors who have gone before them. And that breaks my heart! I pray that spirit will not be the spirit and mindset that we carry, and I pray it will not be the spirit and mindset of my life.

God is a generational God, who sees the end from the beginning and sees the unfolding of His great plan as ONE PLAN, not a patchwork quilt. The culmination of all things is brought together by the history that preceded it. The end of a season wouldn't be an ending if it wasn't followed by a beginning.

Let's be people who train our spirit and our soul to honour those who have gone before us. They gave their lives to position us into the era that we now find ourselves in. Their lives mattered, their steps mattered, their choices mattered–even the bad choices! It all matters and God weighs it all and has taken it all into account.

Mary and Elizabeth are the recipients and carriers of two eras. Mary is the carrier of a Bridge into a wonderful new era. His name is Jesus! And He is the Author and Finisher of our faith Who, for the joy that was set before Him, endured the cross, despising the shame, and He is now sat down at the right hand of the Majesty in heaven.

Finally, I want to say this: environment matters. We see that Mary made haste to Elizabeth's house to share an environment with someone who could relate to her situation, with someone who could relate to what she was going through, to what she was facing.

PROPHETIC WORD

And I hear the Lord's saying in this season, "Make haste for your environment matters! Where you choose to place yourself in this season matters! As you find the right environment, it will cause that which I have placed down on the inside of you to grow and come to life. It will cause that which I placed in the womb of your consciousness, to grow up into all its fullness. For there shall be no dysfunction, and there shall be no toxicity. For it shall grow strong and shall be fed upon the nutrients in the environment and conversation that you are planted within." For the Lord says, "This is a time where I am weeding out those who are not with you but were only in it for themselves. And this is a time where I am attaching you to new relationships that will fuel and feed the new era that I placed down inside your spirit." For the Lord says, "There shall be a leaping within your soul, and there shall be a leaping within your spirit that will serve as a means of confirmation that you are in the right place, at the right time, with the right people. There shall be a supernatural connectedness that you cannot manufacture yourself." And the Lord says, "This is a time where new assignments and new callings are being born. This is a time where new things are coming to light that have been lying dormant within you." But the Lord says, "I am now shedding light on those dormant things, and they shall become the catalyst of opening up a new way for you! They shall be the catalyst in shedding light amid confusion. They shall be the catalyst in bringing peace where there has been confusion. For I the Lord am doing these things in this day and in this hour," says the Lord.

BIRTHING A NEW ERA

Luke 2:1-7

*And it came to pass in those days that a decree went out
from Caesar Augustus that all the world should be
registered. This census first took place while Quirinius
was governing Syria. So all went to be registered, everyone
to his own city. Joseph also went up from Galilee, out of
the city of Nazareth, into Judea, to the city of David, which
is called Bethlehem, because he was of the house and
lineage of David, to be registered with Mary, his betrothed
wife, who was with child. So it was, that while they were
there, the days were completed for her to be delivered.
And she brought forth her firstborn Son, and wrapped
Him in swaddling cloths, and laid Him in a manger,
because there was no room for them in the inn.*

As we enter the landscape of this passage of scripture,
we find ourselves entering it from both a panoramic
view and a grassroots level. We are arriving on the scene

with a broad lens which considers the political and governmental players that are in power at that time. Yet as we narrow our lens, we find ourselves focusing on the true protagonist of the story, and that is Mary, the mother of Jesus, the young woman who is carrying the Messiah within herself.

Even a brief encounter with this moment in biblical history helps us recognise the way the kingdom of God operates in our own lives. It helps us see how God begins to transform towns, cities, and even nations. You see, the kingdom of God often arrives by stealth in seed form on a grass-roots level, planting itself in very ordinary people's lives. However, that does not deny the potency and the power of its significance!

We can see how God in His sovereign wisdom often bypasses the high and mighty and comes to plant His promise in the hearts of those without earthly status, money, or power.

He comes to the weak to put to shame those things which are mighty. He comes to the insignificant and humble and raises them up, bringing to nothing those who are noble and strong in the eyes of the world.

We enter this story at a time of great, upheaval, and movement. Caesar Augustus, the emperor and reformer of Rome, nephew and adopted son of the great Julius Caesar, has just called a global census for everyone under his rule and dominion. He is taking stock of his kingdom by charging everyone to return to their hometowns to be registered.

This is a time when the population is multiplying, and Rome is beginning to feel the pinch in the supply of resources, housing, jobs, and the like. It was a time when Caesar Augustus is reforming and taking account of the economic status of his empire.

Amid this upheaval, we narrow our lens upon a young woman and a young man who have the great responsibility of birthing and parenting the Son of God, and of ushering in a new era into this moment in history!

Now, what we need to understand is that what they were carrying was not to be some kind of a sideshow; this wasn't to be the birthing of something that would remain on the fringes of society. No, what they were about to birth would become the central theme, life source, and heartbeat of God upon the Earth. What they were carrying, had much more weight and significance to it than anyone would give them credit for at that particular time. Nobody saw it and nobody recognised it or deemed it to be valuable–but it was arriving nonetheless!

They didn't need to tweet about it, they didn't need to promote it on Instagram or Facebook... It was arriving despite the lack of understanding and celebration. It was even at the door! And its power and relevance would be backed by heaven, which would be enough.

Let me say this: birthing a new era is not for the faint-hearted. Mary and Joseph's journey was anything but comfortable. From the moment of Christ's conception, there was movement and discomfort in both of their lives. When Jesus was conceived within Mary's womb she was forced to make haste to her cousin Elizabeth's house for safety and respite.

The angel Gabriel had personally visited Mary to announce that she would give birth to the Son of God. The Holy Spirit would overshadow her, and she would conceive. And from the moment the child was conceived, her life was completely disrupted and overwhelmed, with the responsibility of birthing the Son of God into the earth and ensuring that He would be protected and would have safe passage.

Mary is pregnant, and she's now forced to move. She's pregnant and unsettled, she's being provoked on purpose. But little does she know it, God is ensuring that thousands of years of prophetic promises are being fulfilled even down to the detail of where she would be location-wise during Christ's birth.

Some people will never do anything great for God because they're not willing to be inconvenienced. They're not willing to carry the weight and responsibility of birthing something for God. The thought of doing something outside their own desires and personal need is a no-go area. But God is looking for those who are willing to say, like Isaiah, "Here, I am send me! Here, I am use me!" (Isaiah 6:8)

For God to birth something new through any of us, there will no doubt be many challenges for that to happen. Let's not be ignorant of the enemy's devices. The enemy is intent on stealing the seed of God that is planted down on the inside of you, and he will do everything in his power to make sure you abort and fail to give birth to what God has planted within you. But the Bible says, "No weapon formed against you shall prosper." (Isaiah 54:17)

Let me say it again: birthing a new era is not for the faint-hearted! Mary and Joseph had to be willing to be divinely pushed from pillar to post to make this happen. We must have a willingness on the inside of our hearts that says, "Yes, God, I will do Your will." I believe that God wants to unveil to us today the expensive cost both physically, emotionally, and spiritually of birthing His plan into the earth.

PROPHETIC WORD

And the Lord says, "What I'm birthing in this time is not for the faint-hearted. The era I'm ushering in is not for those who are married to comfort or formula." For the Lord says,

"You've never seen anything like this before! This will not be a repeat of old-time legacy. This will not be a repeat of the formulas of the past. This new era is being handed to those who are willing to be misunderstood. This new era is being passed to those who will take steps in the direction that I lead them. And yes, there shall be a separation from the comfort of relationships, from the comfort of towns and even nations, and all that you have been akin to. I'm calling a census!" says God. "I'm calling a gathering together of a new flow and a new sound, and yes, there shall be a falling away from that which you have known and been accustomed to. There will be a weakening and a dissolving of past connections and movements." But the Lord says, "I'm making room for you, and I'm making space for you to flourish... I have gone ahead of you, and I am circumstantially using events to reposition you, to prepare you for the birthing of what I have placed on the inside of you" says God. "I am also gathering together, those who will be the divine connections for this next day, and for this next hour," says the Lord.

Mary and Joseph are on their way back to Joseph's hometown Bethlehem. They are both being pushed and pressed by circumstances beyond their immediate control. Whether we realise it or not God uses circumstances beyond our control to fulfil his purpose in our lives.

BIRTHING A NEW ERA

Before you even got here, God created a predestined plan for you in His sovereign wisdom. All your days were ordained for you, written in His book before one ever came to be. And now you are the embodiment of the plan that He has preordained for you–you are here walking it out!

These things are often difficult for us to understand in our finite understanding of who God is because we think we're making all the decisions and choices. And to a large degree that is true. But God, who is eternal, knows every choice you will ever make, He knows every path you will ever take, and He has a unique way of interrupting and superseding your plans to ensure that He gets you where you need to be, and alongside whom you need to be doing it with.

Mary and Joseph are travelling from Galilee to Bethlehem, which is a ninety-mile journey on foot. Although Mary is on the back of a donkey, let's remember that she's heavily pregnant! Phew!

Now ninety miles in a car is a long way to travel when you're pregnant, let alone being on the back of a donkey in the heat of the Middle Eastern sun! Nonetheless, they are on the road towards Bethlehem.

Mary is in a place of unfamiliar surroundings, as this is not her hometown, but Joseph's. She is heavily pregnant, and most likely exhausted from the journey, and no doubt she's looking for a place to refresh, rest and relax. However, soon after they arrive Mary feels an unusual pressure build-up in her body, and suddenly her waters break, and she goes into labour. I bet Mary is thinking "Oh, no! I mean, come on, God. Not now! This is not the time for me to give birth, not while I'm in transit. We haven't even found a comfortable place to stay yet!"

There's no doubt a mixture of panic, anxiety, and excitement in the air as Joseph is forced to scramble around and find somewhere for Mary to deliver the baby.

Can I let you into a secret? People often say that God's timing is perfect. Ha! Well, it may be perfect to God and possibly perfect to us in hindsight. But oftentimes it's anything but perfect for us at the time. I'd go so far as to say that God has a website called lastminute.com, and it's not for holidays! God will often take you to the brink and cause you to exhaust every other option before He comes through!

And here's Mary; she's in a strange place, through incredibly unusual circumstances (an angelic visitation and then a global census), and now she has nowhere safe and comfortable to deliver a baby. The best thing Joseph can do is find some accommodation immediately, so he finds a local inn and, with his future wife in the midst of labour (possibly screaming in pain) he runs to the door of the inn expecting to hear some good news about finding a room for her to give birth in. But what they find is not good news: they are sadly turned away and told that there is no room at the inn! In other words, "We're full and there's no room for what you're carrying here."

Maybe you're in a place right now where the door has been shut in your face and there's no room for you to birth what's in your heart. Maybe you're in a place right now where you need someone to give you some empathy, compassion and understanding, but you're hard-pressed to find any. Maybe you're in a place today where you're fed up and exhausted and you feel it's necessary to force your way in and make a way for yourself because no one else seems to care. Maybe you think the Lord has forgotten you? But here's what I believe the Lord wants to say to you.

PROPHETIC WORD

The Lord says, "You don't need to force your way into places that I have not pre-arranged for you. You don't need to force your influence into speaking into realms and situations that I've not called for you to speak into. I've shut the door for a reason, because that's not where I want you to birth the promise. Your rejection is simply a redirection." And the Lord says, "Don't waste your time in offence shouting at closed doors, for I am simply moving you towards an open door of opportunity in this new season." The Lord says, "I have a thousand ways to bless you! For your birthing ground shall be different and your birthing ground will not be what you're usually used to." But the Lord says, "It shall be perfect for what I'm about to do. For what you are birthing shall bring change and it shall be a voice of restoration. What you are birthing will transform its surroundings. So rejoice for I the Lord know exactly what I'm doing. And not many days from now you'll see the full weight and impact of what I'm doing. For the shift has started and the time is now. Yes, the baby is kicking in the womb! Yes, the waters have broken, and the push has begun!" And God says, "There shall be spiritual midwives in this hour that I'm sending to gather around you. Those who will help you deliver that which I have placed on the inside of you. They will not be so much a voice of comfort, but a voice of strength. And they shall be a voice of assurance and confirmation. And they will be a voice that encourages you to push!" So, the Lord says, "Get ready to be at home with a season of discomfort! For what I'm bringing to pass, is the birthing of a new era." And the Lord says, "It shall be messy in its arrival, but once you hear its cry, you will know it intimately. And once you see its face, you will know that it was yours all along. There shall be a heart connection to that which I am birthing through you, and there shall be a supernatural reverence and understanding and there shall be a rhythm and a flow." And God says,

"Those who are destined to walk with you and build with you in this hour shall come... And they will complement the moment that you are in. For they will not be disappointed or discouraged by their surroundings. No, they will not be swayed by the era of mess, nor by the era of a needy Child. But they shall come equipped and ready to feed that which I am building. They will be ready to pour their hearts and resources into the blessing of nurturing and growing the future." And God says, *"For what I am doing is not only about fulfilling the promises of those who are equipped and ready for now, but it's also about fulfilling the future promises of those who will carry my promises forward into the next generation,"* says the Lord.

Now the Bible doesn't say if Joseph and Mary were redirected by the innkeeper to a barn where Mary would give birth to Jesus, but I love that God chose a barn in which to birth His Son. Because, for me, this levels the playing field for all of us. God could've chosen to birth His Son through the elite families or power structures of that time, but He chose not to. He chose to birth His beautiful Son through an unknown virgin girl and an unknown young man in an insignificant town called Bethlehem. Not only that–let me say it again–He chose to birth him in a barn!

I believe God wants to let you know today that it's never about the circumstances that surround you, nor is it about the postcode that you were born in, nor is it about the amount of money that you have in your bank account. It's also not about the credentials you have on your reference, nor is it about the labels you wear. It's not about who you know or who you're seen with. No! It's about God's seed of promise, and it's about the heart and life He chooses to plant that seed within.

Because I believe the birthing of this new era is all about God finding the right hearts and Him finding a simplistic faith and a willingness for Him to do what He desires to do. All God is looking for is a YES, and when he finds a YES, He can do great things!

In the discomfort of a barn, God chose to birth a new era. And it may be that the birthing of your new era will be done without the kind of resources you think you need. You might think you need a new computer when all you have is a pen and paper. You might believe you need a comfortable office when all you've got is your garden shed. Wouldn't it be great if you could just have a bigger team to help you fulfil your dream, but all you've got right now is your spouse to help. You might need more sleep because you're working around the clock to make ends meet, but the cost of birthing something is expensive. More sleep will eventually come, but in the meantime, I'm praying God will give you supernatural strength.

And even though Mary gave birth to Jesus in a barn and placed him in a manger (which is an animal feeding trough), it did not deny the power and significance of Christ's life and the weight of His magnificent future.

Friend, God can do great things in strange places, in forgotten places! I don't doubt that in the coming days, weeks, and months, you will see the faces and hear the voices of those who are birthing this new era. They might be in a barn right now giving birth, and it probably won't look pretty! But they are coming.

I hear the sound of footsteps, and I hear the sound of their laughter; I can hear the sound of their faith! They won't be perfect, no! Some of them are far from perfect. But they are the sound of the future, and they won't be armchair critics when they come. They will be cheerleaders and supporters.

PROPHETIC WORD

If you're willing to pour your lives into them, God says, "I will raise them up and they will not disappoint you. If you are willing to invest in them, you will quickly see a return. And your heart will swell with joy when you see them quickly, take what you have given them and multiply it. For they shall have an energy and a vigour about them. And they will carry the excitement of a new time within them. For we are heading into days of divine fulfilment. We are heading into days of answered prayer." For the Lord says, "I have heard the prayers that you have prayed, and they are now being answered." And God says, "All that you have cried out for is now being dispatched for the Word is becoming flesh, and you shall hold it in your arms. For I, the Lord am doing these things in this day and in this hour," says the Lord.

6
A BEAUTIFUL NEW ERA

Acts 3:1-10

Now Peter and John went up together to the temple at the hour of prayer, the ninth hour. And a certain man lame from his mother's womb was carried, whom they laid daily at the gate of the temple which is called Beautiful, to ask alms from those who entered the temple; who, seeing Peter and John about to go into the temple, asked for alms. And fixing his eyes on him, with John, Peter said, "Look at us." So he gave them his attention, expecting to receive something from them. Then Peter said, "Silver and gold I do not have, but what I do have I give you: In the name of Jesus Christ of Nazareth, rise up and walk." And he took him by the right hand and lifted him up, and immediately his feet and ankle bones received strength. So he, leaping up, stood and walked and entered the temple with them–walking, leaping, and praising God. And all the people saw him walking and praising God. Then they knew that it was he who sat begging alms at the

*Beautiful Gate of the temple; and they were filled with
wonder and amazement at what had happened to him.*

Here we find, in my opinion, two of the greatest
apostles and men that ever graced the planet—the
apostle Peter and the apostle John. Both men are incredibly
significant, as they are central characters in the birthing,
pioneering, and establishing of the early church. Both
men had the incredible privilege of living and walking
near the Lord Jesus Christ. They were part of Christ's
team and ministry and were also active partakers and
figureheads during many of the miraculous signs and
wonders that took place during Christ's three-and-a-half-
year, world-shaking ministry. They were eyewitnesses
of a level of life being displayed that only a few have ever
had the opportunity to see, a level of life that would
impact their lives and billions thereafter forever.

We now understand from this passage of scripture
that the baton of succession has been passed to them to
grow and expand that which Christ died and rose again
to birth and usher into the earth—and that is the Church.

Only days before this moment, Peter stood up on the
day of Pentecost to preach the inaugural address to the
church to a large crowd in Jerusalem.

Acts 2:2-4
And suddenly there came a sound from heaven, as of a
rushing mighty wind, and it filled the whole house where
they were sitting. Then there appeared to them divided
tongues, as of fire, and one sat upon each of them. And
they were all filled with the Holy Spirit and began to speak
with other tongues, as the Spirit gave them utterance.

On that monumental day, about three thousand people were saved and the church of Jesus Christ emerged from its fragile state of existence into a stronger more established form. The church community was being built and added to, relationships were being forged, people were praying together, and a vital Church was growing. Signs and wonders were breaking out, Christ was being exalted and something magnificent was taking place!

We now see Peter and John stepping into the fullness of their calling. The bitter sting of Peter's denial of Christ, which once clouded his vision, has now dissipated and passed away. The pain that once gripped the heart of John in the crucifying of his beloved Jesus has now been replaced with a renewed sense of faith, boldness, and action. There is now forward motion within them. There is now power and authority in their words. There is healing in their hands and even healing in their shadow!

This is a great time for the early church, and even though

challenge and resistance are not far from them, it is not hindering the work of the Holy Spirit, for the Bible says the Holy Spirit is not chained, He is everywhere at once, at one time, and no devil, no man, no scheme, and no challenge, can stop the mighty work of the Holy Spirit!

We find Peter and John together on their way to the temple for the hour of prayer. It's the ninth hour–morning–and I'm sure the only thing they have on their minds is to preach Christ to those who are gathering. A large crowd is forming, and I believe that Peter and John are praying for an opportunity. As they walk through the gate of the temple, which is called the Gate Beautiful, a God opportunity presents itself to them.

The Bible tells us, a man lame from his mother's womb is begging at the gate. He's asking for money, for alms, from those who are entering the temple. No doubt he's already received a few coins from those who are passing by, but he's just about to receive a whole lot more than a few coins on this particular day! He doesn't know it yet, but his life is just about to radically change.

You know, I believe there are moments in our life when things radically shift. God has specific things marked out on the calendar of our lives that are designed to usher in change. But often they arrive inside the mundane activities of our lives. They usually arrive when we least expect it, and when they do show up, they have no fanfare, no trumpet blast, and no balloons and song to announce to you that here is a life-changing moment.

God opportunities are usually presented to us in frustrating, painful, lonely, and difficult seasons of our lives; seasons where we feel sidelined and disconnected from the usual rhythm and flow that everyone else seems to be enjoying. God opportunities arrive when we seemingly have no other options, or when our relational infrastructure has shifted and even dried up. I've noticed that God opportunities show up when we're at our wit's end and when there's no other way but for God to make a way where there seems no way!

This lame man was just about to rise into a new era, but he didn't know it yet. I'm here to say that you're about to rise into a new era but maybe you don't know it yet either. The lame man awoke that day with no idea, with no understanding, that he was about to step across the threshold into a brand-new era.

The reality he was experiencing had always been his reality. He was born into it. In other words, he didn't get to choose the environment that he was thrust into from birth.

There are some things in life that we don't get to choose, like who our family is, what our financial status will be when we arrive on earth, our country of origin, what we will look like, our genetic makeup, our weaknesses, proclivities, and frailties. We don't get to choose any of these things.

We can also see that this man was carried and laid daily at the gate of the temple where he begged. This gives us an understanding that this man was helped and positioned in a cycle of behaviour that had become a recurring theme, a stronghold. That's why we need to take responsibility in recognising where our relationships, thoughts, and decisions are carrying us. The reality is, we are all carriers of something that will become a hindrance or help to our future growth, and to those around us. We must choose well.

It's a big decision because God forbid that we should be carried in a direction that we don't want to go. I believe that we often relinquish our future into the hands of someone who carries us somewhere we don't want to go. Someone who carries us into circumstances that we don't want to be in. We say to ourselves, "I don't want to be here, God, I'm better than this! I don't want to be here, God, I'm bigger than this. I don't want to be here, God, this is not working, my heart is breaking. I don't want to be here, God, because I can see something better! I don't want to be here God."

We get a sense that not only was this man physically lame, but he was also spiritually and mentally lame. I believe this to be true because, any time your weakness becomes your means of trade, it tells you that you've sold yourself on the notion that this is your lot.

Some people don't want to move on from their current state of mind or current situation because it has become a means of benefit and provision to them, and changing things would mean disrupting the way they get paid or provided for. They'd rather stay connected to the issue or the weakness and keep banging its drum because it provides a level of life that they are familiar with.

But familiarity can hold you in a lesser version of whom God has called you to be. That's why Jesus walked away from His hometown Nazareth and couldn't do any mighty works there–familiarity was hindering His flow and hindering His ability to operate on a higher level. And when I say higher level, I mean operating in the fullness of His calling.

So, for Jesus to move higher, He needed to position himself in a different environment, around relationships that were able to receive what He carried. Those who were able to embrace Him in the light of who He truly was. Not a dumbed-down version!

The environment and the mindset you're allowing yourself to stay in and be dominated and confined by is what's stopping you from coming into the fullness of your calling or from being fully healed. I'm not so much talking about a physical environment as much as a spiritual environment, although you may need to change both because the lame man certainly needed to change both.

This lame man was a beggar, not by choice but by birth. He was thrust into circumstances that had defined him all his life. And the only way he was going to break out of his current circumstances, into a beautiful new era, was by being offered and embracing a new mindset. Beggars have a certain mindset, and any time we allow ourselves to be a beggar in any area of our life, it will mean that we come across as a victim or as inferior to others. It will mean that we come across as presenting ourselves as less than those whom we are begging from. But Jesus didn't die, shed His blood, and hang upon a cross for any of us to remain a beggar in any area of our lives!

God does not want our weakness to become a negative limitation, a roadblock, or a hindrance to any forward momentum in our lives. The fact is, we all need help in different areas of our lives due to limitations; however, we must be careful and vigilant in not allowing our weakness to forever, define our future or our reality.

Some people don't believe in themselves enough to move on because they've lost hope, so their weakness becomes their normal. They don't have the kind of support system or infrastructure that helps them move on. They lack the kind of relationships that resource, equip and empower them to move on. But that's where the Church can step in and help them rise to a new level of life. But if the Church remains bound then how is the Church ever going to help the bound become free? We need the Church to get free: spiritually, mentally, emotionally, physically, relationally, economically, and the list goes on . . .

Life is a journey, but we need to ask the Lord to help us find freedom in every area of our life so that we can become effective to others. Your victory, in any area of your life, will become someone else's victory if you choose to pass it on. I thank God for the community of faith, for without it I never would have moved on like I did. The Church community is so important! I thank God for friends like Jim 'Dru' Drury who took me in after I got saved from terrible conditions. He fed me, clothed me, and paid for my rent for a month until I regained my physical strength and found a suitable job. I also thank God for the many people who gathered around me and helped to support me in the first few years of my journey with the wisdom of Christ. They steered me in the right direction until I found enough strength to find Christ-dependence and reproduce what had been taught to me.

The Gate Beautiful represents a gate between two realities: where you currently are and where you potentially could be next. It's a transitional place, it's the place of a new you.

This lame man was sitting by a physical gate, and whether you realise it or not you are sitting by a gate too: a spiritual gate. It's a gate that seeks to psychologically interrupt your world and propel you into a beautiful new era. But here's the deal: some people sit by the gate but sadly fail to enter a new reality, because they're not connected to Christ in the way they should be. They have no intimacy with Christ, they don't pray or read the Bible. They are not connected to the body of Christ in a way that introduces them to quality relationships that can encourage them on their Christ-centred journey. They fail to change what God is asking them to change, and this becomes a stumbling block.

Now, that sounds like a criticism, but my friend, it's the truth. We need to invest in ourselves, and we need to invest in our relationship with God. However, in the case of this man, the beggar, he failed to enter in because he simply lacked an opportunity. And Peter and John represent that opportunity, for they are the carriers of a new era for this man.

I believe we need to recognise that God has purposely hidden some of the answers, the promises, and the provision we need in others. Alternatively, some of the answers other people need are stored up in you! God has designed things so that some people who come into our lives are like gate openers.

John 10:7-10 (TPT)

So Jesus went over it again, "I speak to you eternal truth: I am the Gate for the flock. All those who broke in before me are thieves who came to steal, but the sheep never listened to them. I am the Gateway. To enter through me is to experience life, freedom, and satisfaction. A thief has only one thing in mind–he wants to steal, slaughter, and destroy. But I have come to give you everything in abundance, more than you expect –life in its fullness until you overflow!"

Let's remember that Jesus isn't here in the flesh now, but you are! If you are a follower of Christ, you are a representation of Him here on the earth. Therefore, you are the one who has the beautiful responsibility of leading others to the ultimate Gateway: Jesus. Look at what takes place in the Scriptures:

Acts 3:4-6

And fixing his eyes on him, with John, Peter said, "Look at us." So he gave them his attention, expecting to receive something from them. Then Peter said, "Silver and gold I do not have, but what I do have I give you: In the name of Jesus Christ of Nazareth, rise up and walk."

Peter said, "Look at us." So the lame man gave the two disciples his attention, expecting to receive something from them.

The man was expecting to receive a few coins, but Peter and John had something much more exciting to give him. They were going to give him an opportunity to receive a new life! I pray that at this time your expectations wouldn't be too low. I think we can water down our expectations because we get used to receiving on a certain level.

We can see that this man was receiving money from a seated position. I hope that you would shift your expectations and begin to believe God at this time for something much higher, and for something of much more value, not only for you but for your children and for the generations that follow. God does not want us to perpetuate the same outcome year after year. It's time to break free!

Here is the game changer: Peter said to the beggar, "Silver and gold, I do not have, but what I do have I give to you. In the name of Jesus Christ of Nazareth, rise up and walk!" (Acts 3:6) In other words, God is saying, "I know you're asking for what you usually ask for, but this is not a usual time! An opportunity has now come to your door because I know what you really need, and I know exactly what's going to break you out of this recurring pattern and theme. There is enough power existing at this moment to do it!"

Friend, when you finally realise how much power and authority resides within Christ who is within you, the game will truly change. When you begin to realise what you have available to you in Christ, your life will be transformed! When you begin to receive insight and revelation into the covenant promises that you have available to you, in the name of Jesus, you will begin to think differently, you will begin to see and talk differently, and you will begin to live as a child of God and not as a beggar.

Peter said, "Rise up and walk!"

In other words, "Break free from this position! Break free from this mindset! Break free from this experience! You've never walked? You've seen people do it, and you can do it too! There's another level in you, there's a higher quality of life within you that you have not discovered yet. You were not born to stay on this level. You were not born to stay where you are!"

Peter took the beggar by the hand and lifted him up. He gave him a hand-up, not a hand-out. That's powerful! You know, a hand-up repositions you, but a hand-out causes you to stay where you are.

When Peter gave away what was alive inside him, and helped the man up, the man received strength! And not only did he receive strength, but he went out leaping and praising God!

I believe that when we begin to take advantage of God's promises, when we take advantage of the opportunities that present themselves to us, when we become expectant for something beyond our usual pattern to occur, not only will we rise up and receive strength but we will see the hand of the Lord move in such a powerful way that we will begin to leap and praise God! Hallelujah!

God knows there are 'walking and leaping and praising' God levels in us. This lame man was begging a minute ago, but God could see the incredible potential in him. He could see him totally restored. His restoration just needed releasing, it just needed someone to reach out a hand and pull him up to another level of life. Nobody but Peter and John could see this potential!

Let's remember that Peter and John carried a revelation of Christ and an intimacy with Him. A revelation of Christ and intimacy with Him can see things that other people can't see. Everybody else walked past this man, day by day, but God gave Peter and John eyes to see, and they were used by God to change this lame man's life.

Whose answer might you be? To begin with (with the power vested in you) you may be your own answer first.

The lame man was at the Gate Beautiful, and the gate certainly lived up to its name that day. It lived up to its name because two men came along possessing a different mindset that would change the whole trajectory of the beggar's life. A beggar became a prince through God's power. A cripple became a champion! Hallelujah!

Now, I want to finish this chapter with a prophetic

word that God spoke into my spirit. I'm praying this will bless and impact you.

PROPHETIC WORD

God says, "For surely you are standing at the Gate Beautiful today. You are standing at the gate of a new choice. And on this day, I ask you to choose life and take on a new perspective." God says, "For surely some have taken on a perspective of doom and gloom, and they walk in it. But I'm asking you to be aware that you are standing at the Gate Beautiful. You are standing in the place of divine fulfilment, for this is the place of a great change-over. This is the place where I lead you through to victory. This is the place where what you have historically been hindered by will fall to the wayside. For this is the place where you will be led into a different experience altogether."

God says, "Surely you have been burdened and held back by many things, but My hand is reaching out to you on this day to pull you out of that which has held you and bound you. So, rise up and walk in new freedom, rise up and walk in your birthright, rise up and walk in the power that I have invested in you. Rise up and walk as a child of God." And God says, "For surely you shall see a transference of all that

I have placed within you begin to multiply itself. For you shall be a witness of the things that I'm getting ready to do through you. And you will marvel as you go forth in leaps and bounds. You will be a catalyst of My grace in this day and in this hour. No more will you be held by the opinions of yesterday, for I have broken the shackles off you!"

And God says, "You shall beg no more. You shall beg no more for permission, and you shall beg no more for approval. For I the Lord have given you permission, and I the Lord have approved you to go forth into the joy of My promise. You are standing on holy ground. The gate is open, and I will lead you out into blessing, favour, and productivity." God says, "This is the day where it all changes, and this is the hour where I increase you and show you what I am capable of doing. No more shall you be held back; no more will you be in a repetitious cycle or a reoccurring theme. I'm changing your story today; I'm changing the pattern and I'm changing the order. You are now at the front of the line for I have hastened your promise! I've hastened your healing and I've hastened your answer." So, God says, "Walk in a spirit of faith in this hour and expect a harvest of blessing to be yours. For I the Lord am doing a beautiful thing in and through you," says the Lord.

CLOSING

I remember, just after the Covid pandemic, standing at the front of our church having a conversation with a lady whom I have known for many years. Her name is Margery. She and her husband were part of my wife's parents' church for many years, before becoming faithful and active members of our own church when Beth and I stepped out to pioneer a work for the Lord.

Margery and I were talking together after one particular service about the impact that Covid-19 had had on our congregation. Quite a number of people had sadly not returned to the life of the church—mostly young families—and so the demographic had significantly changed. It had therefore become a reality that we would need to rebuild again and find our second-wind.

I remember saying to Margery, "It seems as though a season has ended and another one is about to begin."

Margery responded thoughtfully by saying, "No, Mark, it's not just the end of a season, it's the end of an era and it's the beginning of a new one."

As she spoke, the word 'era' pierced my heart like an arrow! I knew it was the Lord speaking to me. That word would not leave my mind for days, weeks even. It turned out that simple conversation opened up a level of prayer and conversation with the Lord that caused me to journal and learn exactly what an era was and what it meant for us all. It also inspired months of teaching and prophecy that flowed from my heart, and has now become the catalyst for this book.

Through these seven messages you have been a witness to many of the things the Lord shared with me after that short and simple but profound conversation–profound at least for me! It was a lesson to me of how important it is to listen when the Lord is speaking. I'm so pleased I didn't dismiss that conversation, as many of the thoughts and prophecies I have written have blessed me immensely. I have simply shared with you what the Lord said to me first. My prayer is that you would take the words of this book and be strengthened and encouraged by them.

I firmly believe we are standing on the threshold of events and happenings that we have never witnessed before. Covid-19 was the beginning of the global stage being set and, although a sense of anxiety and foreboding remains in the atmosphere, there is also a sense of expectation, godly optimism and hope. I truly believe God has saved the highest level of His glory to be revealed until last!

Romans 8:18-19
For I consider that the sufferings of this present time are not worthy to be compared with the glory which shall be revealed in us. For the earnest expectation of the creation eagerly waits for the revealing of the sons of God.

There is a collision of forces at work in bringing about the will of God to usher in the most glorious and profound transformation (within in humanity and creation) that we have witnessed to date. My prayer is that we, the Church, God's precious sons and daughters, would continue to stand firm on the frontline to pray "God's will be done on earth as it is in heaven."

This is a new era and God has chosen you to be a part of it. What will you do with that responsibility?

PRAYER

Long ago, I made the decision never to take for granted that everyone has prayed a prayer to receive Jesus as their Lord, so I am including this as the finale to this book. If you have never asked Jesus into your life and would like to do that now, it's so easy. Just pray this simple prayer:

Dear Lord Jesus, thank You for dying on the cross for me. I believe that You gave Your life so that I could have life. When You died on the cross, You died as an innocent man who had done nothing wrong. You were paying for my sins and the debt I could never pay. I believe in You, Jesus, and receive the brand new life and fresh start that the Bible promises that I can have. Thank You for my sins forgiven, for the righteousness that comes to me as a gift from You, for hope and love beyond what I have known and the assurance of eternal life that is now mine. Amen.

Get yourself a Bible and maybe start with the gospel John in the New Testament. Start to pray - prayer is simply talking to God - and find a church that's alive and get your life planted in it. These simple ingredients will cause your relationship with God to grow.

ABOUT THE AUTHOR

Mark Stevens is known as one of the UK's leading exponents of praise and worship. Mark has a passion to see people rise up and live out their best life!

After a life-changing encounter with Christ in 1996, which freed him from brokenness and addiction, Mark began to serve and lead worship at Hillsong Church in Sydney Australia. Mark then moved and settled in the UK in 2000 where he married Bethan. He then worked for eleven years as Worship Pastor and Creative Director at Abundant Life Church (now Life Church) in Bradford England.

Mark then launched out as a Creative Consultant, travelling extensively, bringing his experience of Worship Leading, Communication and Team Building to churches and ministries across the UK, USA and Europe.

In November 2017, until the end of 2022, Mark and Bethan had the opportunity to pioneer Rise Church and, over a six-year season, saw many lives impacted in the local community of Leeds, UK.

Towards the end of 2022 Mark's passion to work

creatively with churches and organisations fuelled his recent change in direction. His focus for 2023 is to galvanise teams to reimagine, reengineer and relaunch their work to better serve their vision. In a fast-paced, disruptive and changing world, he believes the church needs to find fresh ways to impact the world.

Mark also continues to lead worship, write songs and loves to communicate the timeless principals of God's Word.

Mark and Beth live in Bradford, England, and have two beautiful children, Jonah and Sienna.

markstevenshome.com

ALSO
AVAILABLE

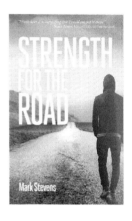

Strength for the Road
by Mark Stevens

'God broke into my world. My life was shaken and transformed instantly.'

These words began the journey of transformation that took Mark Stevens out of a life bound by drug and alcohol addiction and into a new adventure of ministry and leadership that has touched all corners of the globe.

Mark shares candidly his testimony of the excitement and temptation of celebrity fame and lifestyle, the devastatingly destructive effects of addiction, and the overwhelming and transforming power of God's healing and presence. He goes on to share from the many experiences and challenges of worship ministry and church leadership over the past fifteen years.

Strength for the Road is Mark Stevens' first book, written to awaken and stir up the worshipper in each of us, to rise up and embrace the journey ahead of us with faith and boldness. Each of our journeys are different but the truth of God's word and His love remains eternal and everlasting, giving each of us the strength we need - and more - to walk the road God has laid out before us.

"Mark's book is so compelling that I could not put it down!"
Nancy Alcorn, Mercy Ministries International

Visit **markstevenshome.com** for details of all
of Mark's ministry and resources.

Follow Mark on social media:
instagram.com/markstevenshome1
facebook.com/MarkStevensMusic
twitter.com/marklstevens